TO FRACK
OR NOT TO FRACK?

How a Small New York Town's
Decision-Making Process Came Up Short

Ronald R. Fraser, Ph.D.

Foreword by Jason Leifer, Esq., Town of Dryden Supervisor

CHESHIRE & COMPANY
VIEWPOINTS PUBLISHING, INC.

WEST FALLS, NEW YORK

Published by
The Cheshire & Company Viewpoints Publishing, Inc.
7744 Center Road, West Falls, NY 14170
Cheshire_Publishing@roadrunner.com
www.smalltowncivics.com

Cover photography: Ted Auch of FracTracker Alliance. This is a photo of a gas well being prepared for high-volume hydraulic fracturing in Ohio in 2016. Aerial support provided by LightHawk.

Cover Design and Interior Layout by Leslie Taylor
Buffalo Creative Group | buffalocreativegroup.com

Printed in the United States of America
First Edition: June 2018
ISBN: 978-0-692-10476-7
Library of Congress Control Number: 2018904360

Thanks...

...to the many Town of Colden citizens and members of Colden Well Being who took their civic duties seriously during the gas-drilling debate by conducting top-notch technical research, preparing and distributing written materials within the community, attending information sharing meetings, voicing their concerns at town board meetings, participating in opinion surveys and repeatedly petitioning their elected officials to protect their health and safety and the town's precious environment.

"If men were angels, no government would be necessary. If angels were to govern men, neither external nor internal controls on government would be necessary. In framing a government which is to be administered by men over men, the great difficulty lies in this: you must first enable the government to control the governed; and in the next place oblige it to control itself."

James Madison
The Federalist, Number 51
Published in the *New York Packet*, February 8, 1788

--—⊗⊗⊗—--

"Legitimization of political power in a constitutional democracy is achieved by "dividing and subdividing the power once held by a unitary sovereign monarch, until all citizens have come to share in it. Consequently, all share responsibility for the manner in which the power of the one-time sovereign is wielded...And the problem of the citizen's responsibility for government has become at least as important as that of the justification of his obedience to government."

Herbert J. Spiro
Responsibility in Government: Theory and Practice, 1969

--—⊗⊗⊗—--

"It is essential to the maintenance of a democratic society that the public business be performed in an open and public manner and that the citizens of this state be fully aware of and able to observe the performance of public officials and attend and listen to the deliberations and decisions that go into the making of public policy. The people must be able to remain informed if they are to retain control over those who are their public servants. It is the only climate under which the commonweal will prosper and enable the governmental process to operate for the benefit of those who created it."

New York State's Open Meetings Law

CONTENTS

FOREWARD

The fight against hydrofracking for natural gas in New York State was a people-powered movement. While there were several high-profiled activists and politicians who have attempted to take credit for the fracking ban, the real heroes are the residents who live in communities across New York State who supported pro-bono attorneys, local governments and grassroots organizations who worked on the ground to persuade decision makers to protect our drinking water.

Without the broad-based support from residents for local bans on gas drilling and hydrofracking, these communities would never have stood-up to the fossil fuel industry. This was exactly the case in my town, Dryden, New York, which, along with the town of Middlefield, New York, enacted gas drilling bans and were, subsequently, both sued by the fossil fuel industry.

Dryden was not the first town to pass a ban on gas drilling, but we were the first to be sued. At the time I was a member of the Dryden Town Board. The Town Board passed the ban in 2011, after we received a petition containing over 1,600 signatures from residents asking us to ban gas drilling. The petition was circulated by the Dryden Resource Awareness Coalition (DRAC) and signed by residents from all political backgrounds.

The number of signatures collected was greater than the win number that any Town Board or Town Supervisor candidate for local office in Dryden had ever received.

I was involved in the move to ban gas drilling from the beginning when, in 2009-2010, a small group called the Bone Plain group first gathered to discuss how to stop Dryden from being fracked. That group became DRAC and coordinated the 2011 petition. DRAC later assisted the candidates who supported the gas drilling ban in the 2011 local election.

The glue that held the coalition of residents together was a sense of protecting the community from what was a predatory industry. Simply put, people did not want to put their drinking water at risk so that a few residents could profit. By 2011, the public was made aware that fracking was not as safe as the industry said it was, and the industry's unwillingness to post bonds to clean-up any damage they caused made people wary of their willingness to be good neighbors. On top of this, the bad behavior of the landsmen who secured the gas leases for the drilling companies, made it easy for people to see that these companies could not be trusted.

Dryden's gas drilling ban became a single issue that drove the 2011 local election. The anti-fracking slate of candidates won the election in a landslide. Voter turnout was the highest it had ever been in a local election because fracking was such a hot-button issue. The industry lawsuit against the town galvanized support for the anti-fracking candidates.

While I was not on the ballot in 2011, it was clear to me, prior to the petition, that fracking would be the issue driving the election. The board members who were running for reelection were not convinced. They were wary of supporting a ban because the faction that was against the gas-drilling ban was very vocal and, before the Board voted on the ban, insisted that the town would be sued. Supporters of a ban were vocal as well, but until the petition was completed the town appeared to be equally divided between pro-ban and anti-ban constituencies.

The other impediment to passing a gas drilling ban was the town's municipal attorney. This was common across the state because many municipal attorneys were cautious, arguing that the ban would be struck down since the state already occupied the field of regulating gas drilling. Nevertheless, our attorney agreed to draft the ban language. This only occurred after he spent many hours talking to pro-bono attorneys David and Helen Slottje, other municipal attorneys, and me about the feasibility of passing a ban that would withstand a lawsuit. This is how the Frew Run case, which was also about regulating land use to determine where gravel mining could occur in a town, became the legal basis for the ban.

The legal basis for the ban was simple. Municipalities are allowed to regulate land uses, such as where an activity or industry occurs, but the state regulates the practice and means of extraction by the industry. This distinction between regulating the land use versus the means by which companies extract natural gas explains why Dryden's ban was against ALL gas drilling, not just the practice of fracking.

Had the Town Board attempted to ban the practice of fracking, Dryden would most likely have lost the lawsuit because the State Department of Environmental Conservation is authorized by the state legislature to regulate gas drilling practices, such as fracking. For many years people failed to make this distinction. Consequently, most municipal leaders believed that municipalities had no legal basis to ban gas drilling, and litigation-shy municipal attorneys were quick to reaffirm this misconception as well because they too failed to make the distinction.

What ultimately allowed Dryden's Town Board to gain the confidence that passing a gas drilling ban was good policy as well as good politics was the demonstration that there was: (1) a sound legal basis for the ban, and; (2) there was political support for the ban. This recipe was successful in Dryden and the anti-fracking party, the local Democratic Party, was able to use this issue to shift the political landscape in Dryden for the past three election cycles.

Nothing is permanent, and political winds do shift, but the effect of the 2011 election has rippled through to the 2017 election cycle where Dryden saw local Republicans back away from their support for gas drilling in the town. Incredibly, in response to the shifted political landscape, Republican candidates ran as environmentalists, something that they had never done before. While Republicans did not prevail, the shift in attitude is profound.

Not every town saw the success that Dryden saw in 2011 and the fight continues on different development issues. Ironically, some towns use the Dryden precedent to fight solar and wind energy, meaning that the issue of land use still resonates in local elections. The legal precedent set by Dryden's case solidified the legal precedent that municipalities may regulate land uses unless the state has carved out a specific exception. While the urgency for passing local gas drilling bans has passed because the Department of Environmental Conservation has effectively prohibited the practice of fracking for natural gas, municipalities still must confront the issue of energy transmission and production.

The lesson to be learned from Dryden is that in order to build the political will for sweeping change people in power need to be engaged on several fronts. That can be through providing professional advice, communicating with grassroots advocacy groups, and listening to the concerns of average citizens. The bottom-line is that when politicians see that there is a well-organized and engaged voter base in favor of a policy, politicians will respond.

JASON M. LEIFER, Esq.
Supervisor, Town of Dryden

PREFACE

Long ago, a short book written by Roscoe Martin, then a Syracuse University professor, was my introduction into how, and why, small town governments differ from larger municipalities. Since I have lived mainly in larger municipalities, that 1957 book, *Grass Roots: Rural Democracy in America*, provided a lasting image of public life in small towns.

Much later, after moving to the Town of Colden, New York, I began to experience, first hand, the governing process in a small, rural town. Then, when the gas drilling debate heated up in New York State and in the Town of Colden, I had a ringside seat as town officials set out to decide whether to allow, or to ban, high volume "fracking" in the town.

Once the debate ended, I took another look at the *Grass Roots* book and wondered how closely what took place in the Town of Colden compared to Martin's 50-years old description of small town governments. Were these, and many other, passages from Martin's book still an accurate description of small town government?

"Rural government is almost wholly amateur. It is amateur in two senses. First, there are few of the tools of professional

management now widely in use among the larger units…Little government is amateur in the further sense that it is personal, not professional."

"Grass-roots politics frequently involves little public policy; on the contrary, it may be largely of a personal character; and it may indeed be cast in terms of personal loyalty rather than in those terms usually held appropriate to the public arena."

This was the starting point for a closer look at democratic governance in the Town of Colden, New York.

INTRODUCTION

In Search of Democracy In a Small New York Town

More than one-half of the 932 town governments operating in New York State have a population less than 2,800.[1] Originally established to provide simple, close-to-home services in the horse-and-buggy 19th century, how well equipped are today's small town officials when confronting complex, conflict-filled 21st century public policy issues? Do small New York towns confuse supplying routine public services—such as, plowing snowy roads, collecting trash and issuing building permits— with democratic governance?

This case study tracks the actions taken by officials in the Town of Colden, population in 2010 of 3,265, as they struggled to deal with a complex land use decision—to ban or allow the drilling for oil and natural gas in the town using the controversial high volume, hydraulic fracturing (HVHF) drilling technique. How well did the official actions observed in the Town of Colden comply with, or sidestep, traditional democratic principles of effective public administration?

---

1 According to New York State's Comptroller's Office

Why Administrative Principles Are Important

The New York State Constitution grants to every local government, including small, rural towns, the power and responsibility to adopt and amend local laws, to ensure the protection, order, conduct, safety, health and well-being of persons and property within the town. The principles of public administration applied in this study are the democratic means by which public officials fulfil their Constitutional responsibilities. They are the standards against which the actions of public officials can be judged. In addition, these principles ensure the actions of town officials are just, fair and serve the common public interest, not self-serving, private interests.

The American system of government rests squarely on five fundamental principles, each an expression of values that define what democracy is all about:

(1.) <u>Separation of Powers.</u> To avoid concentrating too much power in too few hands and to hold public officials accountable for their actions governmental powers are divided and shared among three independent branches— legislative, executive and judicial—each serving as a check on the actions of the other two branches.

(2.) <u>Rule of Law.</u> To avoid arbitrary and autocratic conduct in office, public officials do not decide what they can and cannot do. Instead, their duties and powers are limited to those specified in applicable laws.

(3.) <u>Workforce Standards.</u> To avoid cronyism in the public workforce, non-elected personnel gain and retain their civil positions based on demonstrated merit and job performance, not political patronage. Public officials have the responsibility to ensure personnel—employees and appointed, part-time, advisors—are sufficiently trained and supervised to perform their assigned duties.

(4.) <u>Due Process.</u> To avoid backroom politics and arbitrary and capricious actions, public decisions are to be conducted in a fair, open and equitable manner, in accord with local administrative laws and administrative procedures.

(5.) <u>Responsiveness.</u> To ensure that public officials are aware of, and responsive to, the concerns of the people—and remain accountable for their actions—every citizen, according to the New York Constitution, may freely speak, write and publish his or her sentiments on all subjects and to assemble and to petition their governments.

When the governing process in a town fails to incorporate these principles, the risk of official misconduct and tyranny goes up. When these principles no longer guide the actions of public officials in New York towns, a democratic government, plain and simple, no longer exists.

What This Study Is, And Is Not

<u>Service-provider Skills</u>. A set of skills currently practiced by town officials—but not a part of this study— involves the supply of a wide array of day-to-day public services experienced directly by the town's citizens, including roadway snow removal, maintenance of the town's roads and the issuance of building permits and dog licenses.

Because these services are readily judged good or bad by the town's citizens—that is, the town's customers—public officials take care to ensure they are conducted well and quickly respond to citizen complaints about poor service.

For two reasons these services are not the focus of this study. First, the Town of Colden does a generally satisfactory job providing these repetitive, routine administrative and operating services.

But more importantly, knowledge of democratic principles are not among the technical skills needed by town officials keeping roadways open during a lake-effect snow storm and issuing dog licenses. In fact, snow removal and road maintenance services are provided equally well in non-democratic systems of government around the world, including communist China and North Korea, a dictatorship.

<u>Democracy-provider Skills</u>. This study will seek answers to these questions: How well do small town officials handle themselves when a non-routine, emotionally charged issue is on the table and the town's population is not unanimous in what it wants their elected officials to accomplish? Do these officials possess the necessary skills to analyze complex policy options, determine which option will best serve their community and then put in place an effective administrative process to reach that goal?

Unlike larger public municipalities, public officials in small, rural towns in New York typically lack public administration training, including the skills needed to apply these democratic principles when dealing with complex, often divisive, public policy issues.

And, since smaller towns typically do not hire experienced staff members with these skills, small town officials are likely to find themselves ill-equipped to handle complex, non-routine policy issues. While they may have the best intentions, many small town officials simply lack a body of knowledge gained by study and experience.

This study looks at what happened when policy makers in one small New York town, the Town of Colden, set in motion a decision making process to decide whether or not to allow or ban companies using HVHF technologies to drill for oil and natural gas in the town.

To what degree were the administrative principles listed above present or absent during the lengthy HVHF debate in the Town of Colden? This complex HVHF decision making process amounted to a test of the sophistication of the administrative skills possessed by Town of Colden officials.

Putting democratic values into the governing process may be less tangible than repairing roadway pot holes, but they are nonetheless essential performance standards for town administrators— especially when they are engaged in making complicated land use decisions with wide-ranging safety, health and environmental consequences for the town's residents.

While this study's unit of analysis is the Town of Colden, I suspect the administrative strengths and weaknesses observed in Colden may very well help citizens and officials in hundreds of other small towns in New York State take a fresh, look at how well their towns are governed.

In addition, this study will potentially fill a gap in the education of public administrators. Eleven colleges in New York State offer curriculums leading to a master of public administration degree. Perhaps because few small towns hire trained public administrators, these courses of study tend to not address, or give short shrift to, the challenges facing public officials in small towns. I hope this study will plug that gap by providing public administration students, even those destined to work in larger municipalities, a better understanding of the governing process in small New York towns.

Methodology. Two sources of information have been relied upon. First, **official meeting minutes** filed by the Colden Town and Planning Boards in the town clerk's office during the HVHF debate were reviewed. These documents provided valuable insights concerning the manner in which the town and planning boards, and their members, performed their duties during the HVHF debate.

In addition, from 2008 to 2014, as a member and chairman, the author enjoyed a ringside seat as a **participant-observer** on the Town of Colden Environmental Board, an official advisory body responsible for providing technical advice to the town board on environmental issues. As a participant-observer present during the HVHF decision making process, I was able to more accurately piece together the events surrounding the town's attempt to grapple with a complex, public policy making event, and to observe, at close range, the behavior of town officials.

My participant-observer role provided important policy making insights not available to an outside observer, including the impact on the decision making process of the town's informal, political/administrative culture—a culture that determined, in part, how town officials made, or avoided making, important HVHF-related decisions.

Finally, as a trained public administrator and researcher, I also bring to the study the skills of a professional policy analyst. These skills include the ability to collect data and track and analyze the actions of town officials as they dealt with HVHF-related issues. As an independent scholar, I have drawn on an educational background that includes a Master of Public Administration degree, a Master of Regional Planning degree and a Ph.D. in Public Policy.

As for practical experience, I served as a senior planner in a federal-state economic development commission for more than nine years and commanded a group of U.S. Coast Guard Reserve search and rescue units along Maryland's Eastern Shore.

A Reader's Roadmap

The Debate. The first chapter provides a brief discussion of the HVHF-drilling process and a timeline of events stretching from 2008 to 2015. The timeline provides an overview of the HVHF-drilling debate in New York State alongside an account of the evolution of the debate in the Town of Colden. Here, in chronological order, are the HVHF-related actions taken by state and local government officials and citizens in the Town of Colden.

Assessing the Debate. Chapters two through five assess the extent to which the actions taken by officials in the Town of Colden during the HVHF-drilling debate were guided by the principles of democratic government.

Chapter six is a summary of ways in which officials can be held accountable for their actions.

What to do? Chapter seven considers a variety of possible options for the future.

CHAPTER ONE

The Gas Drilling Debate in New York State
What is the Fuss All About?

High volume, horizontal, hydraulic fracturing (HVHF), or "fracking," injects a mixture of water, sand, and chemical additives into gas-bearing shale rocks at extremely high pressure to expand and hold open rock fissures and allow the trapped gas to flow out of the shale formations and up the bore hole to the surface. Because these wells go down more than a mile, and then out horizontally for more than a mile in all directions, 10 or more millions of gallons of the chemical-water mixture are pumped underground to frack each horizontal well bore. Then, after each well bore is fracked millions of gallons of the contaminated chemical-water mixture are returned to the surface. A single well may be fractured many times.

Each fracked well requires 600-800 truck trips to deliver water to the well pad, as well as hundreds more trips to haul away contaminated "produced water." Much of this contamination comes from naturally occurring chlorides, heavy metals and radioactivity previously locked in the shale. But the "produced" water also includes fracking fluids – tens of thousands of gallons of industrial chemicals, the composition of which remains a trade secret. As many as 260 separate chemicals are added to fracking fluids, including benzene, toluene, ethylbenzene, and xylene, endocrine disrupters that are dangerous even in small quantities.

The cover photo will give you some idea of the massive, industrial operation of a single, ten-acre, HVHF drilling pad. HVHF-drilling is unlike "conventional," oil and gas wells that simply drill vertically down into oil and gas reservoirs. A state-granted HVHF-drilling permit would establish, for each HVHF well pad, a 640 acre industrial drilling zone in which local town zoning ordinances would no longer apply. Each well requires massive amounts of heavy pressure-generating equipment running 24 hours-a-day; non-stop truck traffic clogging rural roads; and the storage and disposal of millions of gallons of toxic wastes. These industrial-level operations risk contaminating local ground and surface water supplies, air quality and the health of animals and people.

The Fracking Timeline

A statewide debate concerning the benefits and risks associated with the controversial HVHF-drilling technology was well underway in New York State long before the debate found its way onto the Town of Colden's agenda.

TOWN OF COLDEN

NEW YORK STATE

2008-2009: The New York Department of Environmental Conservation began receiving requests from natural gas drilling companies for state-issued drilling permits to explore for gas using the HVHF-drilling technology.

Citizens and environmental advocacy groups, however, began identifying risks associated with the HVHF-drilling operations in Pennsylvania and elsewhere.

The New York Department of Environmental Conservation determined that a new Supplemental Generic Environmental Impact Statement (SGEIS) for HVHF-drilling was warranted. Public hearings were held. The public submitted 13,000 comments on the SGEIS.

July 2010: The New York State Senate passed a HVHF-drilling moratorium bill with a bipartisan vote of 49 to 9.

December 2010: The New York State Assembly passed the fracking moratorium bill with a bipartisan vote of 93 to 43. But Governor David Paterson vetoed the bill and, instead, issued Executive Order 41, a one year moratorium on

NEW YORK STATE	TOWN OF COLDEN
HVHF-drilling in New York State and opened the SGEIS for another round of public comments. **January 2011:** Andrew Cuomo becomes governor of New York State and issued a continuation of Executive Order 41. **February 2011:** Hundreds of concerned doctors, scientists and environmental groups sent a letter to the New York State Department of Health commissioner, Dr. Nirav Shah, informing him of the potential health impacts from HVHF-drilling.	**February 2011:** Colden Well Being formed. This town-based organization—initiated by concerned Colden citizens— was created to protect the town's drinking water wells and other natural resources, personal and community rights, health and the quality of life. Monthly meetings were held, a monthly newsletter published and individual members made short statements at town board meetings highlighting different health and environmental concerns and HVHF-related issues. **February 2011:** Colden Well Being mailed questionnaires to Colden Town Board members asking their individual positions on HVHF-drilling in the town. No responses were received.

NEW YORK STATE

June 2011: The Town of Middlefield enacted a local zoning law prohibiting HVHF-drilling for oil and gas in the town. Cooperstown Holstein Corp., a local landowner, challenged the Middlefield law in court. Lower courts agreed that New York towns have the authority to control land use—but not to regulate oil and gas drilling procedures.

August 2011: The Town of Dryden enacted a zoning amendment that prohibited all oil and gas extraction, exploration, development and related activities within the town. Anschutz Exploration Corp. challenged the Dryden zoning amendment in court.

September 2011: Gov. Cuomo announced the New York State Department of Environmental Conservation decision to allow or ban HVHF-drilling will be based on known facts and science.

TOWN OF COLDEN

May 2011: Colden Well Being held a HVHF-drilling information forum in the town's senior center. Speakers included environmentalists and gas industry officials. Approximately 70 persons attended the event.

June 2011: Town of Wales, a town sharing a common boundary with the Town of Colden, passed a local law banning HVHF-drilling in the town.

September 2011: Colden Well Being members manned a HVHF-drilling information booth at the Colden Arts Festival.

NEW YORK STATE

January 2012: The New York Department of Environmental Conservation receives more than 80,000 comments on the SGEIS.

February 2012: Two separate state Supreme Court (not the state's highest court) decisions upheld the legal authority of the Towns of Dryden and Middlefield to enact land use zoning ordinances banning gas drilling in their jurisdictions, adding that only the New York State Department of Environmental Conservation has the authority to issue regulations, on a statewide basis, controlling how drilling companies operate.

TOWN OF COLDEN

April 2012: Town of Colden passes its first six month moratorium on HVHF-drilling stating, the town "has under review a Local Law governing the use of horizontal drilling and hydraulic fracturing for gas exploration...[and that] drilling in the rural environment of the Town of Colden violates the rights of residents and imposes a significant threat to their health, safety and welfare."

NEW YORK STATE	TOWN OF COLDEN
	Ed. Note: *With this action town officials publicly announced they had "under review a Local Law governing the use of horizontal drilling and hydraulic fracturing for gas exploration." According to the town's own ethics law, Chapter 11, Section 4E of the Town of Colden Code titled, Disclosure of Interest in Legislation, town board and planning board members, from this date, were obligated to publicly disclose, on the official record, the nature and extent of any direct or indirect financial or other private interests they have in such legislation.* **April 2012:** Colden Well Being held a second HVHF-drilling information forum at the Bread of Life church. Approximately 60 people attended. **April 2012 Colden Planning Board Meeting Minutes:** The planning board reviewed the Town of Holland's proposed HVHF-drilling law but concludes that a similar law in the Town Colden "could be potentially restrictive to current wells and individual residents."

NEW YORK STATE

TOWN OF COLDEN

July 2012 Colden Town Board Meeting Minutes: A Colden Well Being member addressed the town board and submitted, on behalf of concerned citizens, a twelve page summary of HVHF-drilling issues as they pertain to the Town of Colden. Her remarks, as recorded in the meeting's minutes, included,

"Many of your constituents wonder where all the members of the Town Board stand on the issue of high volume slick water hydraulic fracturing...it is important for all to have just a little more time to look at the literature and research your point of view.

"Did you ask the pro-bono law firm, CEDC Law [Community Environmental Defense Council] to assist with extending the moratorium? If not, why not? Did you request that the Planning Board and the Environmental Board study the issue of hydrofracking as it relates to the Town of Colden and provide feedback? What were the results?"

NEW YORK STATE

TOWN OF COLDEN

July 2012 Colden Planning Board Meeting Minutes: "A lengthy discussion ensued regarding the current approach to the issue of gas drilling in the Town....Concern was raised regarding the rights of individual land owners regarding existing leases, existing wells, as well as future drilling....there might be a silent majority that has not come forward in favor of continued exploration and drilling."

Ed. Note. *Contrast the concerns contained in the town board's April 2012 drilling moratorium, community-wide environmental, health and safety concerns, with the planning board's concern that a ban on HVHF-drilling could restrict a few town landowners who currently operate gas wells on their property and those who may want to operate gas drilling wells in the future.*

August 2012 Colden Planning Board Meeting Minutes: Discussion of how to proceed with consideration of a HVHF-drilling law for Colden took place "but no consensus resulted other than to await the 13 September Town Board meeting that may reveal the direction the Town wishes to

NEW YORK STATE	TOWN OF COLDEN
	take regarding drilling operations in Colden,"
	August 2012 Colden Town Board Meeting Minutes: At a public hearing to discuss the town's pending second six-month HVHF-drilling moratorium, "…11 residents commented with their concerns with the Local Law extending the Moratorium on Hydrofracking and Horizontal Drilling."
	One citizen submitted, in addition, a six-page discussion of the risks associated with HVHF-drilling as well as other liability issues, such as the availability of home owner insurance and mortgages on properties with HVHF-drilling operations.
	August 2012: Since the town's planning board had failed to adequately address the HVHF-drilling issue, as requested by the town supervisor, the Town of Colden supervisor establishes an ad-hoc Hydrofracking Committee to study HVHF-drilling issues and "compile a list of zoning concerns to be incorporated into our zoning ordinance."

NEW YORK STATE	TOWN OF COLDEN
	(Disclosure, the author was appointed to chair this committee)
	Among the first acts of the Hydrofracking Committee, each committee member filed a written disclosure of his or her financial and other interests in the oil and gas industry. These disclosures were then filed with the town's clerk.
	August 2012: The Town of Holland—also a town sharing a common border with the Town of Colden—passed a local law permitting HVHF-drilling in the town.
September 2012: The New York Department of Environmental Conservation asked the New York Department of Health to review the SEGEIS.	**September 2012:** Colden Well Being members again provided a HVHF-drilling information booth at the Colden Arts Festival and gathered signatures for its anti-HVHF-drilling petition.
September 2012: By a 95-40 vote, the Democratic-controlled assembly passed a moratorium that would ban fracking in New York until May, 2015. A similar bill failed to reach the floor for a vote in the Republican-controlled Senate.	**September 2012:** Colden Well Being sent a mail survey to all homes in the Town of Colden asking whether residents are in favor of, or opposed to, HVHF-drilling in the Town of Colden. (See Appendix B for a copy of the survey instrument)

NEW YORK STATE	TOWN OF COLDEN
	Survey response: 400 residents responded that they are opposed to HVHF-drilling in the town. Three residents favored HVHF-drilling in the town.
	October 2012: Town of Colden passed a second six-month HVHF-drilling moratorium in the town, stating, the town "has under review a Local Law governing the use of horizontal drilling and hydraulic fracturing for gas exploration…[HVHF] drilling in the rural environment of the Town of Colden **MAY** violate the rights of residents and imposes a significant threat to their health, safety and welfare."
November 2012: The New York Department of Environmental Conservation published its final draft HVHF-drilling regulations.	
November 2012: According to FracTracker Alliance, 54 towns and villages in New York State—many located along the New York/Pennsylvania border— have acted to officially allow HVHF-drilling in their jurisdictions.	

NEW YORK STATE	TOWN OF COLDEN
January 2013: The New York Department of Environmental Conservation received over 260,000 comments on its proposed HVHF-drilling regulations—almost all opposed.	**April 2013:** Town of Colden passed a one year HVHF-drilling moratorium in the town, stating, the town "has under review a Local Law governing the use of horizontal drilling and hydraulic fracturing for gas exploration… [HVHF] drilling in the rural environment of the Town of Colden **MAY** violate the rights of residents and imposes a significant threat to their health, safety and welfare."
March 2013: New York Assembly passed a two-year HVHF moratorium.	During a public hearing held prior to adoption of the moratorium, the *Springville Journal* reported that the town's supervisor defended the moratorium by saying, "We're just trying to protect everybody in the town." The town's code

NEW YORK STATE

TOWN OF COLDEN

enforcement officer's response: "There are certain people that you're taking their rights away from. That's what you have to remember. You're not protecting big landowners."

April 2013: Drawing on its nine-month long review of the environmental and health risks associated with HVHF-drilling, and the policy guidance provided by the Town of Colden's master land use plans, gas industry research, interviews with gas industry officials, discussions of HVHF issues with Colden citizens, and a series of monthly working meetings, the Colden Hydrofracking Committee submitted its report, *Gas Drilling in the Town of Colden: A Report to the Colden Town Board & All Colden Citizens,"* to the Colden Town Board with this recommendation:

"The committee finds that the known land use impacts associated with high volume, hydraulic fracturing (HVHF)—a wide area, heavy industrial operation—are incompatible with the land use and community values promoted in the Town's adopted master plans and zoning ordinance. We recommend that the Town's zoning

NEW YORK STATE	TOWN OF COLDEN
	ordinance be amended to prohibit both HVHF-drilling activities for oil or gas, and the disposal of HVHF waste fluids from elsewhere, in the Town of Colden. We further recommend that vehicles transporting such fluids and wastes be prohibited on Town roads."
	Ed. Note: *The Hydrofracking Committee report (accessed January 18, 2018) is posted on the Town of Colden website at: townofcolden.com/site/wp-content/uploads/2014/05/ Gas-Drilling-Report.pdf*
	May 2013: Colden Hydrofracking Committee presented its report to members of the town board at its regular monthly workshop. Workshop minutes noted: "the report was excellent, very informative and well done."
	May 2013: Town of Colden town supervisor sent a memo to the planning board chairman, dated May 5, referring the Hydrofracking Committee's report to the Planning Board, with this request: "The Town Board would like to see the Planning Board prepare recommendations for a zoning

NEW YORK STATE

TOWN OF COLDEN

ordinance as it pertains to HVHF and the Town of Colden's Master Plans…"

Ed. Note. *See Appendix F for the entire memo.*

June 2013: Colden Planning Board Meeting Minutes:
"The Planning Board will continue to study the issue of gas development and HVHF. The Planning Board will review all options including the possible application of a special use permit with regard to future gas development."

June 2013: Drawing on the language found in the Town of Middlefield's court-tested local law banning HVHF-drilling, the Hydrofracking Committee submitted draft zoning code amendment language to the Town Board.

July 2013: Colden Planning Board Meeting Minutes:
"The Planning Board continues its Town Board requested review of the Hydrofracking Committee's report….A motion to accept the recommendations of the HFC report was made but not seconded" by another planning board member and the motion died.

NEW YORK STATE	TOWN OF COLDEN
	August 2013: Colden Town Board terminated the Hydrofracking Committee stating in its letter that, "The Planning Board plans to utilize the data and facts outlined in the report to fulfill their responsibility to recommend legislation to the Town Board."
	August 2013 Colden Planning Board Meeting Minutes: "The chair stated that the board has been advised by several parties that the issue of hydrofracking is not an emergency and that we should wait for the New York Department of Environmental Conservation to set some regulations and decide at that time if they are acceptable to us as a town… for now we should research alternatives and wait to see a draft from the New York Department of Environmental Conservation."
	Ed. Note. *The planning board's wait-and-see approach was, apparently, driven by the expectation that the state would, in fact, decide to issue pro-HVHF drilling regulations, followed by issuing HVHF-drilling permits. This, of course, never happened.*

NEW YORK STATE	TOWN OF COLDEN
	At this meeting, a planning board member stated that "he feels the board is shirking its responsibilities by not seconding the (July 2013) motion [to accept the Hydrofracking Committee's report recommendations] and that it means we are not considering the findings of the report."
	Ed. Note. This is the last meeting of the planning board at which the Hydrofracking Committee's report is mentioned in meeting minutes. The planning board essentially ignored the supervisor's May 5th request for its recommendations to amend the town's zoning ordinance based on the findings contained in the Hydrofracking Committee report.
	September 2013: For the third year, Colden Well Being members operated a HVHF-drilling information booth at the Colden Arts Festival.
	October 2013: Colden Well Being members presented their HVHF-drilling slideshow to the entire community at the Bread of Life church.

NEW YORK STATE	TOWN OF COLDEN
	November 2013: Prior to the November election, a challenger for the position of town supervisor (subsequently elected to the post) promised that if elected, he would let the towns' people decide whether the town should ban or allow HVHF-drilling in the town.
	April 2014: Town of Colden passes a second one year HVHF-drilling moratorium in the town, stating, the town "has under review a Local Law governing the use of horizontal drilling and hydraulic fracturing for gas exploration…[HVHF] drilling in the rural environment of the Town of Colden **MAY** violate the rights of residents and imposes a significant threat to their health, safety and welfare."
	April 2014: The Chairwoman of the Colden Environmental Board submits to the Town Board the Environmental Board's adopted recommendation to ban HVHF-drilling in the town and a list of proposed changes to the town's zoning ordinance to put the ban into effect. These proposed ordinance amendments drew upon the language found in

NEW YORK STATE	TOWN OF COLDEN

NEW YORK STATE

June 2014: New York's top court, the Court of Appeals, affirmed the rulings of lower courts that the Town of Middlefield, the Town of Dryden—and all New York towns—have the legal authority to regulate land use within towns and to enact zoning laws prohibiting HVHF gas drilling. The court specifically examined and accepted the zoning language found in the Towns of Middlefield and Dryden zoning laws.

October 2014: According to FracTracker, 85 New York towns, cities and villages have acted to officially ban HVHF-drilling in their jurisdictions.

Ed. Note. *With the passage of time and the availability of more information concerning the risks associated with HVHF-drilling, the number of municipalities acting to ban HVHF-drilling increased.*

TOWN OF COLDEN

the Town of Middlefield's law banning HVHF-drilling—language affirmed by lower courts.

October 2014: The new Town of Colden supervisor sent a mail survey to all homes in the town, stating, "As your supervisor and town board members prepare to address the issue of high volume hydraulic fracturing within the town limits, we want to give town residents the chance to have their voices heard." (See Appendix C for a copy of the town's survey instrument.)

Survey response: 232 residents against HVHF-drilling in the town; 19 residents favored HVHF-drilling in the town.

NEW YORK STATE

December 2014: At a cabinet meeting held in Albany, and attended by Governor Cuomo, New York Department of Health acting commissioner, Dr. Howard Zucker, issued the department's report, *Review of High Volume Hydraulic Fracturing for Shale Gas Development*, stating that: "…the overall weight of the evidence from the cumulative body of information contained in this Public Health Review demonstrates that there are significant uncertainties about the kinds of adverse health outcomes that may be associated with HVHF….Until the science provides sufficient information to determine the level of risk to public health from HVHF to all New Yorkers and whether the risks can be adequately managed, DOH recommends that HVHF should not proceed in New York State."

At that cabinet meeting Department of Environmental Conservation Commissioner, Joe Martens, said he would

TOWN OF COLDEN

October 2014: Colden Well Being's HVHF-drilling informational booth at the Colden Arts Festival collected an additional 52 anti-HVHF-drilling signed surveys.

December 1, 2014: The author filed, in the Colden Town Court, an Official Misconduct charge against the chairman of the Colden planning board. (See Appendix F)

December 2014 Colden Town Board Meeting Minutes: "Town Supervisor requested that the Town Board come to a resolution next year on Horizontal Drilling and Hydraulic Fracking [since] the [town's] moratorium will end in March 2015."

December 2014-January2015: A member of Colden Well Being, sent the Colden Town Board emails that (1.) stressed the need for town board members to "…fully disclose their financial interests in a fracking decision…" and (2.) drawing on the advice received from David Slottje, an experienced, pro-bono, HVHF-drilling attorney at the Community Environmental Defense Council in Ithaca, NY,

NEW YORK STATE

issue a final SGEIS findings statement next year prohibiting HVHF-drilling in New York State.

Governor Cuomo thanked the commissioners and their departments for their work.

TOWN OF COLDEN

pointed out why the Town of Colden's proposed HVHF-drilling ban, prepared by the town's local attorney, is deeply flawed and will not protect the Colden community from the risks associated with HVHF-drilling.

Ed. Note. *In response to this citizen-review of the town's draft HVHF law, the town supervisor responded with an email that read, in part, "This [the draft HVHF law] is only a work in progress draft and will be reviewed by our boards. Perhaps you should have applied for one of the openings on the boards if you wanted to have input prior to a public hearing."*

Not only did the town deny citizen input during the formative stages of the decision-making and law-drafting process, the town board did not consult, at no cost, with Mr. Slottje, an expert in HVHF-drilling law.

January 2015 Colden Town Board Meeting Minutes: The Town Supervisor stated: "At last month's meeting [I] mentioned to the Town Board the issue of Hydrofracking within the Town. Since our last meeting New York State

NEW YORK STATE

TOWN OF COLDEN

has come forward and made a decision that Hydrofracking is not a safe practice for the state and **passed a Law banning Hydrofracking in New York State** (emphasis added). The Supervisor still feels the Town Board should make a decision on the way the Town of Colden looks at Hydrofracking."

"The supervisor submitted a draft of a Local Law on prohibiting the use of High Volume Horizontal Hydraulic Fracturing to the Town Board to review and copies will be given to the Planning and Environmental Boards for their review as well."

Ed. Notes. *The supervisor's January 2015 declaration that the state had passed a law banning HVHF-drilling is untrue. The State of New York legislature has never passed a bill banning HVHF-drilling in the state, and the governor has never signed such a bill into law.*

Six months later, in June 2015, based on the SGEIS review and the Department of Health report, the New York Department of Environmental Conservation, a state agency,

NEW YORK STATE

TOWN OF COLDEN

issued the state's "Finding Statement," concluding that the department would prohibit HVHF-drilling in the state by not issuing HVHF-drilling permits.

Since there is no state law to protect the Town of Colden, at any time the New York Department of Environmental Conservation could, based on new HVHF-drilling studies, reverse its decision and begin issuing HVHF-drilling permits in the state—and in the Town of Colden.

The only permanent protection against the risks associated with HVHF-drilling in the Town of Colden, is the enactment of a local law banning HVHF-drilling in the town.

January 2015 Colden Planning Board Meeting Minutes: In response to the town board's request for a review of the town attorney's draft local HVHF law, the minutes read: "State brought down law, why pile on local ordinance—Redundant."

Ed. Note: The planning board is also under the illusion that there exists a New York State law banning HVHF-

NEW YORK STATE	TOWN OF COLDEN
	drilling in the state, and used this erroneous information to suggest a Town of Colden HVHF-drilling ban—a real law—is not needed.
	February 27, 2015: A meeting was held in the town hall between this study's author and the Colden Town Supervisor to discuss required public HVHF-related disclosures by town officials.
	The supervisor presented a folder containing copies of annual financial disclosure forms prepared by members of the town and planning boards. These state-required declarations are filed to disclose relationships between town officials and vendors doing business with the town of Colden.
June 2015: The New York State Department of Environmental Conservation issued its official "Finding Statement" for the department's *Final SGEIS on the Oil and Gas and Solution Mining Regulatory Program*, stating that:	The author responded that these state-mandated disclosures do not satisfy the requirements of Chapter 11, Section 4E of the Town of Colden local laws and he noted that members of the town board and planning board have been considering local legislation that would impact the oil and gas industry since April 2012. Since members of both boards have failed to comply with Colden's own town
"In the end, there are no feasible or prudent alternatives that would adequately avoid or minimize adverse environmental impacts and that address the scientific uncertainties and risks to public health from this (HVHF) activity. The Department's chosen alternative to prohibit high-volume hydraulic fracturing is the best alternative based on the balance between protection of the environment and public health and economic and social considerations."	

NEW YORK STATE	TOWN OF COLDEN
	ethics law by not publicly disclosing to the citizens of the Town of Colden their interests in the oil and gas industry, they have been in violation of this local law since April of 2012.

The author noted that New York State Department of Environmental Conservation records show that during this period at least two members of the Colden planning board have maintained gas wells on their property, an apparent, undisclosed, conflict of interest.

With this, the supervisor became defensive. To avoid non-compliance with the town's own law, he said he would withdraw the draft Colden HVHF-drilling ban and the town will depend on the [non-existing] state law to protect the people of Colden. With that apparently arbitrary and capricious decision, the supervisor ended the meeting.

This is also where the town's efforts, since April 2012, to decide whether a HVHF-drilling ban was in the best interest of the town, ended. The town's policy-making process was simply unable to deal with this complex public issue. |

CHAPTER TWO

Separation of Powers

PRINCIPLE: To avoid concentrating too much power in too few hands, and to hold public officials accountable for their actions, governmental powers are divided and shared among three independent branches—legislative, executive and judicial—each serving as a check, a restraint, on the actions of the other two branches.

* * * * *

America's Three-Branch Government Model

The all-American, three-branch government design—including independent legislsative, executive and judicial branches—is a key component of democratic-style public administration.

While the three branches are designed to act independently of one another to hold public officials accountable, functionally, they form three parts of a single, governing whole. A well-operating, democratic government depends on checks and balances but also on how well each branch contributes to the overall governing process.

Every high school student learns that in America the powers

exercised by federal, state and local officials are to be limited by a system of checks and balances among the three branches of government. Here is a passage from a typical high school textbook, *Government Alive: Power, Politics and You,* read by students from the Town of Colden attending the Springville Griffith Institute located in the Village of Springville, Erie County, New York:

"The Constitution divides power in the national government among the three separate branches. This separation of powers was a key component in the framers' vision of limited government. James Madison wrote, 'The accumulation of all powers, legislative, executive and judiciary, in the same hands...may justly be pronounced the very definition of tyranny.'"

"The framers took this principle a step further by inserting provisions in the Constitution that would allow each branch to check, or limit, the power of each of the other branches."

In practice, these so-called power-limiting checks include: the ability of the executive branch to veto bills passed by the legislature; the legislature's power of approval and oversight of executive branch spending plans; and a judicial branch empowered to rule on the legality of executive branch and legislative branch actions.

Federal Government

In Washington, for example, a federal court ruled that the House of Representatives has the authority to sue President Obama, claiming his administration's health care subsidies to insurance companies are not legal. Why? Because these expenditures were not specifically appropriated by the legislature for that purpose.

New York State

The three-branch model in Albany includes: a two-chamber legislature consisting of the Assembly and the Senate; an elected governor serving as the chief executive of a 160,000-person executive branch; and a unified, statewide court system.

Governor Cuomo's January 2017 veto of a bill passed by the state legislature transferring certain legal costs, then borne by counties, to the state, is an example of how the executive branch checks the legislative branch in New York State.

Erie County

Erie County's three-branch government includes a single chamber, 20 member, county legislature; an elected executive officer in charge of the county's 4,000-person executive branch; and the statewide, unified court system.

In July 2016 Erie County executive, Mark Poloncarz, vetoed a legislature-approved bill proposing changes to the county's charter. Poloncarz told the *Buffalo News* that he opposed the bill because it would weaken his authority over the county attorney's office and strengthen the legislature's power by extending legislators' terms in office from two to four years.

The introduction of the three-branch model in Erie County is a relatively recent event. The Erie County Legislature's website (accessed January 20, 2018) tells us that, "Up until 1961, legislative and executive powers in Erie County were combined in the Board of Supervisors...[but]...With the adoption of the Charter [form of government in 1959], Erie County established a traditional form of legislative, executive and judicial separation of powers which is *common to all other levels of government.*" (Emphasis added)

Well, not all level of government. Let's take a look at the Town of Colden.

Town of Colden

Unlike both New York State and Erie County, the Town of Colden's government structure—and the government structure likely to be found in many other small towns in New York State—do not follow the traditional three-branch model.

The Town of Colden does elect a town supervisor and four

councilpersons to its legislative, law making body, the town board. But that is where any resemblance to the three-branch model ends.

New York State's Department of State, in its *Local Government Handbook*, tells us, "The [New York] Town Law does not provide for a separate executive branch in town governments. Because the supervisor occupies the leader's position on the town board, and because town residents often turn to the supervisor with their problems, many people think the supervisor's position is the executive position of town government. But the supervisor is part of the legislative branch and acts as a member and presiding officer of the town board. He or she acts as a full member of the board, voting on all questions and having no additional tie-breaking or veto power."

By law, the town supervisor is assigned a few additional duties, including, as the town treasurer, to account for the town's monies and sell, lease and convey town properties when directed by the town board. These enumerated administrative duties do not, however, raise the status of the town supervisor to that of a one-person executive branch of government, or even to the status of the town's executive officer.

The *Local Government Handbook* adds: "The [State] Legislature has authorized towns to adopt local laws superseding many specific provisions of the Town Law. The purpose of this legislation was to allow towns to restructure their form of government to provide for an executive or administrative branch separate and apart from the legislative branch of government." Larger towns in New York State, including the Town of Amherst in Erie County, have created an executive branch.

The widespread absence of an independent executive branch of government in small towns, a key part of the three-branch model, is lost and with it a means of holding the town board members accountable for their actions. This knocks one leg out from under the three-branch model by eliminating an independent town executive branch staffed with trained officials capable of both conducting business in accordance with democratic principles and challenging, where appropriate, actions of the town board. While this safeguard is found in both the Erie County and New York State governments, it is absent in the Town of Colden.

But, since all New York towns already have the legal authority to create an executive branch, officials in the Town of Colden have purposefully decided that they prefer the status-quo: the concentration of power in a single branch.   Because the Town of Colden does not operate with an independent executive branch, the same five, part-time members of the elected town board—the town's law making body—are also responsible for overseeing the execution of its own laws and the delivery of the town's legislature-approved services and programs.

The Judicial Branch

At first glance, town-level courts in New York give the illusion that the third leg of the three-branch model is at work in New York towns. Upon closer examination, this is not quite the case.

The Town of Colden Justice Court is part of the New York State Unified Court System. In its publication, *Justice Court Manual*, the Unified Court System both promotes the need for three independent branches of government, but it also makes it clear that local town Justice Courts do not have the authority to serve as an effective check against improper actions taken by the town's legislative branch.

The *Manual* tells us, "Preserving separation-of-powers among the executive, legislative and judicial branches is essential to our system of government. The United States Constitution and the New York State Constitution both require that no one branch of government be allowed to dominate the others: only by each branch fulfilling its proper roles can the three branches together 'check and balance' each other....Judicial independence and its protections are core features of the separation of powers, and apply as much to towns and villages as to other levels of government."

Still, in a section of the *Manual* titled, "Town and Village Courts," we find that the Colden town court is really not empowered to function as a check on the actions of the Colden town board, the town's legislative branch:

"In general, Justice Courts are empowered to hear both civil and criminal cases, but are courts of limited jurisdiction in that they adjudicate only certain types of civil and criminal cases. On the civil side, Justice Courts hear money actions that do not exceed $3,000...On the criminal side, Justice Courts are local criminal courts with...the power to adjudicate misdemeanor and petty offenses, and arraign defendants in felony cases before they are transferred to a superior court.

"While Justice Courts have limited jurisdiction...each Justice Court is responsible for administering justice consistent with the Constitution and its separation of powers..."

Regarding the enforcement of town enacted laws, the *Justice Court Manual* reads: "Violations of town or village laws or resolutions, which are subject to civil penalties not exceeding $3,000 per event, also can be heard in the local Justice Court. Justice Courts, however, do not have the power to grant provisional remedies such as injunctive powers, relative to town and village ordinances."

Without the injunctive power, the Colden Town Court is unable to check questionable actions of town officials. Since the town court is not in the business of holding town officers accountable, another leg of the three-branch model is lost leaving the people of the Town of Colden without the protection promised by the American separation-of-power principle.

In other words, the Colden Town Court can help the town board enforce town laws and ordinances against town citizens (e.g., zoning, traffic and dog licensing) but it cannot order the town officials to stop an action that may be unlawful, unethical or otherwise harmful. Why is this important? The separation-of-powers principle depends on the judicial branch of American governments to have the power, when petitioned to do so, to step in, and if justified, halt questionable legislative and executive branch actions.

In response to a 2017 Freedom of Information request asking how frequently the Town of Colden court receives cases involving the town government, or members of its staff, as defendants, the Colden Court Clerk replied, based on her personal tenure at the court: "To the best of my knowledge and recollection, there have not been any cases against the Town of Colden Municipal Office and/or their staff filed with the Town of Colden Court, since April 2015 to the current date [November 10, 2017]."

To be fair, the Colden Town Court depends on town citizens and county local law enforcement officers, in conjunction with county prosecutors, to bring cases alleging misdeeds before the court. Citizens seldom initiate legal challenges against the actions of town officials and, a senior detective, a 30-year veteran in the Erie County Sheriff's Office, acknowledged that the Sheriff's Office does not usually get involved in local government performance issues. In fact, in a telephone interview, he could not recall knowing of such a case.

If the Colden town court is not in the business of holding the town's public officials accountable, what does the court do?

Of the 365 cases initiated in 2015, 273 involved vehicle traffic offences in the town, 30 cases involved New York Penal Code offences, 20 were parks and recreation cases and 19 involved local law cases.

Of the 282 cases initiated in 2016, 231 involved vehicle traffic offences in the town, and 33 cases involved New York Penal Code offences.

In 2017 the Town of Colden initiated, as the plaintiff, 12 cases against citizens involving laws regulating dogs. In 2016 the Town of Colden initiated 46 cases involving laws regulating dogs.

To sum up, the Founders' three-branch model of checks and balances, a protection against abuse of power in public agencies, has been abandoned in the Town of Colden. What takes the place of the all-American three-branch model of government is a one-branch unit of government that concentrates, unchecked, all political and administrative powers in a single five-member body.

Why do many small New York towns favor a form of government that places so much power in the hands of so few officials?

One explanation is offered by the New York Department of State's Division of Local Government Services. On its website (accessed on January 20, 2018) we learn:

"There are 1607 general purpose local governments in New York State, each with its own governing body and taxing authority. These have evolved in response to legislative initiatives enacted when residents wanted to be physically close to their elected representatives because travel was time-consuming and arduous…these considerations may no longer be relevant, yet we retain the legacy of a fragmented and unsustainable system of governance."

An October, 2006 report from the Office of the New York State Comptroller, titled, *Outdated Municipal Structures: Cities, Towns and Villages, 18ᵗʰ Century Designations for 21ˢᵗ Century Communities,* adds these historical insights:

"The vast majority of our cities, towns and villages were established prior to 1920. Overwhelming changes have occurred in the built environment, demographics and economy since that time, but there has been no corresponding adjustment in underlying municipal structure or boundaries…

"Starting from scratch, no expert or group of experts would design the 'system' of local government operating in New York State today…Ironically, the last major change to the rules of the game—the municipal home rule and annexation changes enacted in 1963—generally served to preserve the existing geographical municipal structure."

In a 1990 report by SUNY New Paltz Professor Gerald Benjamin, titled *The Evolution of New York State's Local Government System*, Benjamin, seeking an explanation for the outdated structure of local government in New York, concludes: "Governance arrangements are sustained by the inertia always attendant to the status quo; by the stake large numbers of local officials have in them; by sentimental attachment in local populations to government entities that may well no longer be needed; and by patterns of state aid to local governments based upon traditional legal categories rather than more appropriate criteria."

CHAPTER THREE

Rule of Law

PRINCIPLE: Public officials do not decide what they can and cannot do. Their duties and powers are limited to those specified in applicable laws.

* * * * *

Long before passage of its first HVHF-drilling moratorium in April 2012, thereby setting in motion a decision-making process to either allow or prohibit HVHF-drilling in the town, the Town of Colden enacted two local laws that should have guided the town's decision-making process.

Ethical Conduct Law

The April 2012 moratorium bought town officials time to study the risks associated with the HVHF-drilling technology before deciding what to do. But it also included this sentence: "The Town Board of the Town of Colden has under review a Local Law governing the use of horizontal drilling and hydraulic fracturing for gas exploration." With that sentence members of the town board and the town's planning board officially became engaged in a policy making process with future ramifications for oil and gas drilling companies.

One might expect, upon enactment of this drilling moratorium, the attention of the town supervisor, town attorney and the town code enforcement officer would have been drawn to the legal disclosure requirement found in Chapter 11 of the town's adopted laws, known as The Code.

Chapter 11, Section 4E of the Town of Colden Code is titled, "Disclosure of Interest in Legislation," and reads: "To the extent that he knows thereof, a member of the Town Board and any officer or employee of the Town of Colden, whether paid or unpaid, who participates in the discussion or gives official opinion to the Town Board or any other official board or agency on any legislation before the Town Board or any other official board or agency shall publicly disclose on the official record the nature and extent of any direct or indirect financial or other private interest he has in such legislation."

This law was not passed to benefit town officials. It was passed to ensure the citizens living in the town would know whether or not the actions of their elected and appointed public officials reflected the interests of the entire community, or the self-serving private interests of members of the town board and the planning board.

The April 2012 drilling moratorium triggered Chapter 11, Section 4E. Thereafter members of the town and planning boards were bound to publicly announce to the town's citizens their ties to the oil and gas industry. But that never happened.

Since a decision by the town board to allow HVHF-drilling in Colden would potentially harm both the wellbeing of the town's citizens and its environment, the people of Colden had a legitimate right to know whether or not the Colden officials involved in making the HVHF-drilling decision had personal ties to the oil and gas industry—ties that might bias their decisions in favor of the oil and gas industry and put the citizens at risk. Lack of enforcement of the disclosure law during the period 2012 to

2015 effectively withheld this important information from the people who needed it most—the town's citizens.

Importantly, during this HVHF-drilling debate, while the Colden planning board was formally in the business of supplying the town board members trustworthy HVHF-drilling advice, state Department of Environmental Conservation records showed that two members of the planning board maintained gas wells on their property. This apparent conflict–of–interest was never publicly disclosed to the people of Colden.

Since April 2012, to the date of this study, the Colden town board and the Colden planning board have failed to file the disclosures called-for in Chapter 11, Section 4E of the Town of Colden's Code—leaving citizens of Colden to wonder: Did the town and planning boards' actions with regard to HVHF-drilling in the town serve the welfare of the community at large, or were these actions taken to serve the personal interests of members of the planning board?

How can the failure to enforce this local town law—and the rule-of-law principle—be explained? On paper this should never have happened. Chapter 28 of the Town of Colden Code, titled, "Building Inspector and Enforcement Officer," reads, in part:

"A. Building Inspector…shall administer and enforce all of the provisions of laws, ordinances and regulations applicable to the construction, alteration, repair, removal and demolition of building and structures…

"B. Enforcement Officer. As Enforcement Officer, he shall enforce all rules, regulations, ordinances and local laws of the Town of Colden."

The formal administrative mechanism for enforcement of the disclosure requirement looked good—on paper. The town's enforcement officer is charged with enforcing all local laws. But in practice, this enforcement mechanism was simply a façade, not the real thing. Could it be that in small towns—where multiple family members may serve on town boards, and where the law makers and the law enforcers are neighbors—loyalty to friends trumps loyalty to the rule-of-law principle?

Passing a law establishing an ethical standard for town officials is the easy part. Mustering the administrative skills and managerial backbone to put the ethical standard into practice—that is, to enforce it—is not. In the absence of an independent executive branch in the Town of Colden and a trained town manager to implement town laws, Colden officials were unable, or unwilling, to enforce the town's ethical standard on members of both the town board and the planning board.

A review of the official meeting minutes for the Colden town board and the planning board from April 2102, to 2015, reveals that not once did either board discuss the public disclosure requirement called for in Chapter 11, Section 4E.

Duties of the Planning Board

A May 5, 2013, memo (See Appendix F) from the Colden town supervisor to the chairman of the Colden Planning Board forwarded the Hydrofracking Committee's report and asked that, "...the Planning Board prepare recommendations for a zoning ordinance as it pertains to HVHF and the Town of Colden's Master Plans."

The Hydrofracking Committee report recommended amending the town's zoning ordinance to prohibit HVHF-drilling in the town, and it reads, in part:

"The committee finds that the known land use impacts associated with high volume, hydraulic fracturing (HVHF)—a wide area, heavy industry operation—are incompatible with the land use and community values promoted in the Town's adopted master plans and zoning ordinance. We recommend that the Town's zoning ordinance be amended to prohibit both HVHF-drilling activities for oil or gas, and the disposal of HVHF waste fluids from elsewhere, in the Town of Colden."

[A copy of the Hydrofracking Committee report (accessed

January 18, 2018) is found at: *townofcolden.com/site/wp-content/ uploads/2014/05/Gas-Drilling-Report.pdf*]

One might expect that upon receipt of the town supervisor's memo and the recommendations found in the Hydrofracking Committee's report, including a recommendation to amend the town's zoning ordinance, would have drawn the attention of members of the planning board and the town's code enforcement officer to Chapter 108-130B, of the town Code that lists the duties of the planning board upon receipt of a proposed amendment to the town's zoning ordinance.

Chapter 108-130B, reads, in part: "Each proposed [zoning] amendment ... shall be referred to the Town Planning Board for an advisory report prior to the public hearing held by the Town Board. In reporting, the Town Planning Board shall fully state its reasons for recommending or opposing the adoption of such proposed amendment and, if it shall recommend adoption, shall describe any changes in conditions which it believes makes the amendment desirable and shall state whether such amendment is in harmony with a master or comprehensive plan for land use in the town."

Chapter 108-130B offered the citizens of Colden the illusion that their planning board's review of the Hydrofracking Committee report would be thorough, technically rigorous and support the land use guidance found in the town's master land use plans. But, in practice, the law only gave the citizens a false confidence that the actions of the planning board would reflect the interests of the entire community, not the private, self-serving interests of a few large landowners.

In addition, on April 7, 2014, the Chairwoman of the Colden Environmental Board submitted to the Town Board its recommendation to ban HVHF in the town and included a list of proposed changes to the town's zoning ordinance to put the ban into effect. These proposed amendments drew upon the language found in the Town of Middlefield law banning

HVHF-drilling—language affirmed by New York courts.

A review of the official meeting minutes of the Colden planning board following the passage of the town's first six-month HVHF-drilling moratorium in April 2012, reveals an official town advisory body focused more on protecting the few land owners with gas wells currently on their property, and the landowners' ability to drill in the future, than on the potential risks HVHF-drilling posed for the safety and health of the town's citizens.

April 2012 planning board minutes: The planning board expressed concern that a law banning HVHF-drilling, "could be potentially restrictive to current wells and individual residents."

July 2012 planning board minutes: "Concerns raised regarding the rights of individual land owners regarding existing leases, existing wells, as well as future drilling…there might be a silent majority that has not come forward in favor of continued exploration and drilling."

Then after receiving the supervisor's May 2013 request for a review of the Hydrofracking Committee's report, the planning board's minutes reveal a lack of interest in providing the town, and its citizens, a competent analysis and report, as requested by the town supervisor.

June 2013 planning board minutes: "The Planning Board will continue to study the issue of gas development and HVHF."

July 2013 planning board minutes: "The Planning Board continues its Town Board requested review of the Hydrofracking Committee's report…A motion to accept the recommendations of the HFC report was made but not seconded."

August 2013 planning board minutes: "The chair stated that the board has been advised by several parties that the issue of hydrofracking is not an emergency and that we should wait for the DEC {Department of Environmental Conservation) to set some [state] regulations…"

This August 2013 meeting of the Colden planning board ended its non-review of the town's Hydrofracking Committee report. From that date forward the planning board minutes never again mention the Hydrofracking Committee report— effectively stonewalling the town supervisor's request that the planning board provide the town, its officials and its people, with a technically reliable review of that report, and prepare recommendations for a HVHF zoning ordinance amendment.

Not only did the planning board fail to comply with a local town ordinance calling on it to supply the town with competent technical advice during the town's HVHF-drilling decision-making process, the Colden planning board also failed to serve the people of Colden by not drawing on additional, state-granted powers contained in New York Town Law, Sections 271 and 272-a, which read, in part:

"Among the most important powers and duties granted by the legislature to a town government is the authority and responsibility to undertake town comprehensive planning and to regulate land use for the purpose of protecting the public health, safety and general welfare of its citizens."

"The planning board shall have the power and authority to employ experts…"

"The planning board may recommend to the town board regulations relating to any subject matter over which the planning board has jurisdiction under this article or any other statute, or under any local law or ordinance of the town."

Since a HVHF-drilling zoning ordinance amendment must be in accord with the town's adopted master land use plan, it is noteworthy that during the entire 2012-2015 period, there is no indication in the planning board's meeting minutes, or elsewhere, that the planning board members reviewed the town's master land use plan. This is but one more example of how ill-trained—or simply unwilling—the Colden planning board members were to carry-out their town and state prescribed duties and provide trustworthy HVHF-drilling advice to the town's law making body.

CHAPTER FOUR

Public Workforce

PRINCIPLE: To avoid cronyism in the public workforce, non-elected personnel gain and retain their civil positions based on demonstrated merit and job performance, not political patronage. Public officials have the responsibility to ensure personnel—employees and appointed, part-time, advisors—are sufficiently trained and supervised to perform their assigned duties.

* * * * *

How well prepared—skill-wise—were members of the Colden planning board for addressing the challenges they faced during the HVHF-drilling debate? First, some history.

In America, the principle that public officers should be sufficiently skilled to perform their assigned tasks got its start in 1883 with the passage, in Washington, of the Civil Service (Pendleton) Act. This statute called for federal jobs to be filled with "open, competitive examinations for testing the fitness of applicants for the public service...[and]...fairly test the relative capacity and fitness of the person examined to discharge the duties of the service into which they seek to be appointed."

New York State followed the federal lead with Article V, Section 6, of the New York State Constitution that reads: "Appointments and promotions in the civil service of the state and all of the civil divisions thereof, including cities and villages, shall be made according to merit and fitness to be ascertained, as far as practicable, by examination which, as far as practicable, shall be competitive ..."

While this section of the state's Constitution speaks directly to civil service employment in New York municipalities, by reference, it also establishes a broader administrative principle that all public servants in the state—including non-civil service officials in small towns—should possess the skills to carry out their assigned duties.

Land Use Planning in New York State

New York towns, in the early 1900s, were classified as involuntary subdivisions of the state for providing "the convenient exercise of government functions by the state for the benefit of all its citizens." Towns became independent local governments, in part, with the granting of home rule powers in 1964, including the power to regulate private land use.

As the land use responsibilities of New York towns became more and more demanding, and town planning boards were called-upon to fulfill technically more complex responsibilities, the need for better training of planning board members became evident.

It is worth repeating here the crucial role of land use planning in New York towns, by citing once again New York Town Law, which reads: "Among the most important powers and duties granted by the legislature to a town government is the authority and responsibility to undertake town comprehensive planning and to regulate land use for the purpose of protecting the public health, safety and general welfare of its citizens."

Prior to 1992, the State Land Use Advisory Committee, a part of the New York State Legislative Commission on Rural Resources in Albany, reported that a high percentage of planning board members lacked training in the "basic procedures which successful use of state and local planning and zoning laws require." This prompted the Commission to introduce in the state legislature a bill to specifically authorize city, town, village and county governments to establish training standards for members of their planning and zoning boards. That bill became law in 1992.

However, a January,1996, SUNY at Buffalo report, *Governance in Erie County: A Foundation for Understanding and Action*, found that town planning board members continued to remain ill-equipped to do their job:

"It should be noted," the report concludes, "that nowhere [in New York State laws] is it required that planning be administered by professionals. As a condition of appointment, planning board members need not have any planning experience, opening the way for appointments that are primarily political. In most jurisdictions in the county [Erie County] there are 'non-professional' planners serving 'non-professional' boards... In the vast majority of smaller towns and villages these activities of planning and zoning remain essentially volunteer efforts of citizen review, recommendation, and regulatory oversight."

And a decade following passage of the 1992 law authorizing towns to establish training programs for their planning boards, the New York State Commission on Rural Resources reported that: "Except for a few noteworthy efforts...little was done by most municipalities to establish formal training requirements and opportunities for members of their planning and zoning bodies...Hence, leaders and members of local government associations, the professional planning community, public and private sectors represented on the State Land Use Advisory Committee came to the realization that the general lack of formal preparation of members of local planning and zoning bodies for their specialized roles and responsibilities was a growing and serious problem that would only become worse unless further state legislative action was taken."

In response, the New York State legislature passed a second bill, signed into law by the governor and became effective in 2007 requiring planning and zoning officials to receive a minimum of four hours of training each year.

To help local officials understand the intent and content of the new law, the New York State Legislative Commission on Rural Resources, in cooperation with the New York Planning Federation, the Association of Towns of the State of New York, the New York State Department of State, the New York Builders Association and the New York Farm Bureau published a two-page "Fact sheet," that included this guidance:

"The new law allows municipalities a wide latitude in training opportunities they may authorize members to receive...The legislative body for each city, county, town or village approves a course or courses of training for its board members...Training opportunities could include courses offered by a municipality, a regional or county planning office, a state agency such as the Department of State, a state association like the Association of Towns, Conference of Mayors or the NY Planning Federation... municipalities should establish a system for keeping track of training received by board members."

In addition, to further help town officials implement the new law, the New York State Department of State issued its own guidance in 2007:

"Planning boards and zoning boards of appeals members make decisions of major importance to their communities... The governing body of each town, village, city or county determines what courses, training providers and training formats are acceptable...governing boards are encouraged to pass resolutions approving training from trusted providers..."

What might an effective planning board training program look like? Since most rural governments in New York State do not employ professional planners New York's Department of State offers a wide range of high quality land use planning courses to boost the skill level of rural planning board members.

Here is a partial list of available Department of State courses offered in 2016 and presented by Department of State planners and attorneys at conferences and workshops across the state: Comprehensive Planning; Ethical Standards for Planning and Zoning Boards; Local Regulations; Enforcement procedures; Planning & Zoning, an Introduction; Planning Board Overview; Public Meetings & Hearings; Rural Planning and Sign Regulations.

The new law did not specify the basic knowledge and skills planning board members need to carry-out their duties, nor did it establish a procedure to hold town boards accountable if they fail to make sure their planning board members are well-trained.

What the law, and the flow of follow-up guidance did do, however, is to establish that town board officials are responsible for providing planning board members well-designed, town board approved, courses of training from trusted providers.

Once again, as in the past, success of the new law depends entirely on the willingness of elected town board members to take their planning board training responsibilities seriously, and to take responsibility for the quality of the advice town boards receive from their planning boards. Obviously, only well-trained planned board members can provide trustworthy land use planning advice. Why would town board members knowingly rely on undependable advice from their unprepared planning boards when making important land use decisions that put at risk the welfare of the citizens they were elected to serve?

Planning Board Training in the Town of Colden

While the Colden planning board exists to provide reliable technical land use planning advice to the Colden town board—advice that will help the town board fulfil its Constitutional duty to protect the health, safety and welfare of the town's citizens—it is the Colden town board's responsible for providing an effective course, or courses, of instruction to ensure the town's planning board members are, in fact, so equipped to provide technically reliable land use planning advice.

Instead of providing town officers and town citizens a carefully prepared analysis of the possible risks to the town and the environment from HVHF-drilling, the Colden planning board focused on the need to protect a few landowners currently maintaining gas wells in the town (including two members on the planning board) and their ability to drill future wells using HVHF technologies. In addition, the planning board was either unable, or unwilling, to comply with the town supervisor's request for a review of the proposed zoning amendments contained in the Hydrofracking Committee's report.

The Colden planning board's unsatisfactory performance stands out in sharp contrast to the HVHF-drilling analysis and advice made available to the town board from other sources, including:

o The citizen-based Colden Well Being, its presentations to town board members, its many well-researched, HVHF-related emails sent to the town board members, community-wide HVHF-drilling information forums and it members' public comments delivered at monthly town board meetings;

o The Environmental Board's written recommendation to amend the town's zoning ordinance to prohibit HVHF-drilling and proposed amendment language;

o Two surveys of the citizens of the Town of Colden, one conducted by Colden Well Being and another conducted by the town, both showing overwhelming support for a town ban on

HVHF-drilling; and

 o The town's Hydrofracking Committee report.

What might explain the planning board's failure to perform its duty during the HVHF-drilling debate?

Since two members of the planning board, according to state Department of Environmental Conservation records, maintained gas wells on their property during the HVHF-drilling debate, the planning board's behavior might be explained as a simple case of private, self-interest overriding the welfare of the community.

Or, perhaps by successfully stonewalling the town supervisor's call for a review of the Hydrofracking Committee report, the planning board members sought to avoid the possibility that the town might adopt a HVHF-drilling ban.

Or, due to poor training and a failure to take their civic duties seriously, the planning board members were unable to muster the technical and analytical skills needed to carry out their responsibilities.

Planning Board Training After 2007

How closely did the training received by the Colden planning board members, after 2007, conform to the training requirements initiated by the 2007 law and the follow-up training guidance offered by both state and private land use planning organizations? Did the Town of Colden adopt an effective, top-down, town board approved course of instruction from trusted providers? While a review of the Colden town board meeting minutes does not provide an answer to these questions, a review of the Colden planning board meeting minutes does.

⁕ ⁕ ⁕ ⁕ ⁕

June 17, 2008 planning board minutes: "TVGA Consultant, architecture and engineering firm in Buffalo, to hold training sessions in Concord for PB members. Two, two-hour sessions will fulfill training requirement."

January 20, 2009 planning board minutes: "Attached is 1/6/09 memo from the Erie County Planning & Environment Department regarding available on-line training courses."

January 19, 2010 planning board minutes: "A planning board member is willing to share training info to help make training more effective and involve a local provider. Another planning board member is reported to have said that he will not attend any sessions regarding working more effectively with others and finds self-evaluation not necessary."

February16, 2010 planning board minutes: "A guest speaker provides a one-hour presentation on historical preservation."

June 15, 2010 planning board minutes: "A training session to be held on June 16th at the Niagara Community College. See chairman for details."

July 20, 2010 planning board minutes: "August meeting to be a training session on confronting NIMBY [Not in my backyard]."

August 17, 2010 planning board minutes: "Maybe a training session is possible in the Town of Holland."

September 21, 2010 planning board minutes: "In November a planning board member will give a one hour session on hydrofracking."

January 18, 2011 planning board minutes: "The chairman is looking for training session ideas from the planning board."

September 17, 2013 planning board minutes: "Chairman announces a lecture will be held at Canisius College on hydro-fracking. There is an upcoming training session at Erie County Community College."

July 2014: The planning board chairman arranged a private meeting—no public notice given—with pro-HVHF-drilling officials from the New York Independent Oil and Gas Association, an oil and gas industry lobbying organization. The emailed meeting notice, with the subject line, "Training," was sent to members of the town board, the planning board and the town's code enforcement officer. No member of the planning board, however, formally submitted this "training" event to the town clerk for credit against his or her 2014 four-hour training requirement.

October 21, 2014 planning board minutes: "Chairman says there is potential training at BOCES in Salamanca."

January 19, 2016 planning board minutes: "Travel dollars available for planning board members to attend relevant training sessions."

These training-related planning board minutes from 2008 to 2016, suggest that:

1.) The concept of a basic course, or courses, of instruction, adopted and approved by the Colden town board, and targeting the identified skills and knowledge board members need to effectively perform their duties, is totally absent.

2.) Instead of a well-designed, top-down course of instruction, the town's so-called training events add-up to a bottom-up, random, catch-catch-can scheme with one aim—to allow planning board members, at their own discretion, to get their annual training tickets punched.

3.) Planning board training in the Town of Colden completely lacked crucial elements of a valid training program, including: the identification of the members' skills needing improvement; and the identification of a coherent course of study capable of achieving these skill-building goals.

4.) The Colden Town Board abandoned their public management responsibilities to ensure that the citizens of the town are served by competent public officials.

5.) Rather than adopt and implement an effective planning board training program, the town board allowed planning board members to conduct a ticket-punching scheme that avoided any serious attempt to ensure the planning board members are capable of delivering reliable land use planning advice to the elected town board, and the citizens of the town.

Appendix E reveals that while one or two planning board members tried to personally take their planning board responsibilities seriously, most did not.

In my professional judgement, no trained public administrator would knowingly appoint to a planning board, even on a part-time, advisory basis, persons lacking the knowledge and skills to perform his or her assigned duties and then, to make matters worse, fail to provide the training resources and courses of instruction needed to ensure the appointees become competent members of the planning board and able to render trustworthy land use planning advice.

CHAPTER FIVE

Political Responsiveness

PRINCIPLE: To ensure public officials are aware of, and responsive to, the concerns of the people—and remain accountable to the people for their actions—every citizen, according to the New York Constitution, may freely speak, write and publish his or her sentiments on all subjects, and to assemble and to petition their governments.

* * * * *

The citizens of the Town of Colden repeatedly expressed, in various ways, what they expected from their local, elected law makers during the HVHF-drilling debate.

April 2013: The town's Hydrofracking Committee sent its report to the town board calling for a ban on HVHF-drilling.

May 2013: The citizen organization, Colden Well Being, surveyed all town citizens with an overwhelming response to ban HVHF-drilling in the town.

May 2013: The Hydrofracking Committee presented its report calling for a ban on HVHF-drilling to the town board.

June 2013: The Hydrofracking Committee sent proposed

zoning ordinance amendment language banning HVHF-drilling to the town board—language recently confirmed by New York courts.

March 2014: According to the *Springville Journal*, at the town's public hearing to gather comments on a proposed local law extending the gas drilling moratorium one year, citizen comments included:

"A lot of us don't have county water. I would be real worried for that."

"I want to keep Colden alive and healthy."

"I would like to see you pass the moratorium tonight, so we are safe for another year."

"Some residents feel their rights would be infringed upon if they could not use their land for hydrofracking."

April 2014: The Colden Environmental Board sent its recommendation to ban HVHF-drilling in the town, to the town board, along with proposed zoning ordinance amendment language.

October 2014: A town-sponsored survey of the citizens of Colden overwhelmingly called for banning HVHF-drilling in the town.

January 2015: At the town's monthly meeting, according to the town board's meeting minutes, the town supervisor submitted a draft local law "to prohibit the use of high-volume horizontal hydraulic fracturing in the town." He added that "Since our last meeting New York State has come forward and made a decision that Hydrofracking is not a safe practice for the state and passed a Law banning Hydrofracking in New York State… [but]…he still feels the Town Board should make a decision on the way the Town of Colden looks at Hydrofracking."

(New York State's legislature and governor never enacted a law banning HVHF-drilling in the state. Nor has the town corrected this error by informing the town's people that the supervisor's statement was misleading and that no such law exists.)

What happened next demonstrates how quickly small town responsiveness can turn into a form of small town authoritarianism.

In early February 2015 town board members received review comments regarding the town's draft HVHF-drilling law from both members of Colden Well Being and other citizens. In addition, one Colden Well Being member provided the town board a detailed, well-researched, rewriting of the town's draft law emphasizing the use of court affirmed HVHF-drilling prohibition language.

These citizen reviews of the draft law claimed: (1.) its language, unlike court-affirmed language used in the Towns of Middlefield and Dryden, would not protect the town from risks associated with HVHF-drilling and, (2.) that the draft law, contrary to recent court decisions, would wrongly give the town the power to regulate how conventional vertical, non-HVHF-drilling companies must operate in the town—a regulatory power vested only in the state.

These comments from citizens regarding a pending town policy with far reaching consequences for the town's citizens generally went unacknowledged by town hall officials.

The final straw took place at a February 27, 2015 meeting at which the town supervisor reneged on his campaign promise to let the people of Colden decide whether or not to allow HVHF-drilling in the town.

When confronted with the failure of members of the town board and planning board, since 2012, to publicly disclose their relationships with the oil and gas industry, the supervisor, in a moment of personal defensiveness, responded that he would remove the draft HVHF-drilling law from further consideration and thereby end the need for the town's officials to file oil and gas disclosure statements.

The town chose to not enforce its own ethical standard—a law to ensure the town's citizens would be informed of potential conflicts of interest among the town's frack-or-no-frack decision makers.

That final, arbitrary decision—when added to a town structure that concentrates, unchecked, power; a poorly trained planning board; and apparent conflict of interest among planning board members—ended the town's ill-fated attempt to address a complex land use issue—to frack or not to frack.

CHAPTER SIX
Holding Public Officials Accountable

In small New York towns lacking formal institutional safe-guards—such as separation of powers and an independent, well-trained executive branch—the responsibility for holding public officials accountable falls more heavily upon the citizens themselves.

In larger municipalities, in the City of Buffalo, for example, investigative reporting by a variety of media—three television networks, the daily *Buffalo News*, weekly papers, *The Public* and *ArtVoice*, and the independent watchdog, Investigative Post—routinely expose questionable actions of public officials.

But this public service is generally not available in smaller towns. The actions of public officials in the Town of Colden, and in many other small towns, seldom receive media attention aimed at holding public officials accountable for their actions.

What, then, are the means available to citizens to hold their public officials accountable for their actions?

Ballot Box. If displeased with the way elected officials perform in office, the next election gives voters an opportunity to replace incumbent office holders.

But the ballot box, as an effective accountability tool, works best in larger municipalities where at least two active and competing political parties are ready to use the next election to highlight the need to replace underperforming incumbents and put forward, on the ballot, more qualified candidates.

In the Town of Colden, and in many small, rural New York towns, this method of holding officials accountable can break down. When Republican-registered voters greatly outnumber registered Democrats—and the town's Democratic Party is poorly organized and not equipped to challenge incumbent office holders—Republican endorsed candidates are readily re-elected, year after year.

Of course, in small towns where registered Democrats greatly outnumber registered Republicans, the same breakdown of accountability at the ballot box is also likely to take place.

VOTER REGISTRATION – NOVEMBER 2017

TOWN NAME	REGISTERED REPUBLICANS	REGISTERED DEMOCRATS
COLDEN	989 (59%)	685 (41%)
HOLLAND	894 (62%)	546 (38%)
SARDINIA	941 (69%)	420 (31%)
WALES	865 (61%)	548 (39%)

Source: New York State Board of Elections

Citizen Engagement. Public officials are held accountable when citizens organize around a public issue and exercise their rights of speech, petition and protest. During the debate over whether the Town of Colden should ban the use of HVHF-drilling for oil and natural gas in the town, the citizen-based organization, Colden Well Being, was formed to study the HVHF-drilling issue and provide town officials with informed, well-researched advice.

In this case, the effectiveness of citizen engagement is

unclear. Colden town officials generally ignored HVHF-drilling advice from members of Colden Well Being and other citizens. At one point the town supervisor suggested that a vocal member of Colden Well Being apply for appointment to the town's planning board or environmental board if she wanted to have a voice in the HVHF-drilling decision making process.

The Courts. Another alternative for holding public officials accountable, although the least preferable, is the courts. To formally challenge an administrative action of a town official in a local town court is both a cumbersome and time-consuming remedy. But even more troublesome, courts tend to focus, rightly, on the legal interpretation of the statute. Did the official's action violate the law, or not, period.

The main purpose of holding public officials to account for their actions, however, is not to establish guilt or innocence according to the law, but to expose the existence of the questionable administrative actions—and to prompt steps to prevent future occurrences.

The lesson here is clear. The courtroom is not a substitute for the ballot box, citizen engagement, media attention and public opinion. But, when these preferred means of accountability fail, a court action may be justified.

On December 1, 2014, the author filed an Article 195, Official Misconduct, complaint in the Colden Town Court against the chairman of the Town of Colden planning board. (See Appendix F for details).

On February 8, 2016 the Town of Boston court and the Erie County District Attorney declined to prosecute, and the case was dismissed. Why? According to the District Attorney, the Colden supervisor's May 13, 2013 memo requesting that the town's planning board review the Hydrofracking Committee's report and provide the town board recommendations for amending the town's zoning ordinance, did not include a date-certain by which the planning board was to fulfill the request. The District

Attorney concluded that in the absence of a due date for rendering the planning board's report to the town board, the planning board chairman could not be charged with Official Misconduct.

To the court, due to an administrative oversight, failure to set a due date for a report from the planning board, the board's chairman could not be legally charged with official misconduct. In other words, the absence of a due date, not the actual poor performance of the planning board, decided the case.

CHAPTER SEVEN

Where To From Here?

During a two-year long effort to decide whether allowing HVHF-drilling is in the best interest of the town, Colden officials were unable, or unwilling, to muster the administrative and political will—even after two surveys showed overwhelming support for a HVHF-drilling ban—to either adopt a policy allowing HVHF-drilling in the town, or adopt a policy banning HVHF-drilling in the town.

In the end, the town failed to carry-out its land use control responsibilities—one of a town's most important duties. Instead, Colden officials forfeited, surrendered, to a state agency, the Department of Environmental Conservation in Albany, their municipal home rule power to protect the safety and health of their citizens.

The findings of this study can be summarized as follows: When judged against four basic principles of American public administration, the HVHF-related decision making actions of officials in the Town of Colden came up short. The tools needed for democratic governance were simply not there.

<u>Separation of Power</u>. In place of a separate, independently-operated executive branch, the Town of Colden government

concentrates power in a single, five-person legislative branch, setting, in part, the stage for the HVHF-drilling policy-making breakdown. In the absence of an executive branch, with a competent town administrator in-charge, relevant town laws were not put into effect and the planning board was not prepared to perform their HVHF-related duties. (Chapter 2)

Rule of Law. By failing to enforce local town laws, town officials—and importantly, the town's citizens—were denied ethical transparency and timely, accurate technical advice from their planning board. By ignoring their own laws, Colden town officials placed themselves above the law. (Chapter 3)

Planning Board's Role. A lack of training among planning board members, and an apparent conflict of interest among planning board members, rendered the town's planning board unable to provide the town board members with trustworthy advice. (Chapter 4)

Responsiveness. In spite of two town surveys expressing overwhelming support for banning HVHF-drilling in the town, and the town supervisor's campaign promise to let the people decide the HVHF-drilling issue, the town arbitrarily aborted consideration of its draft law banning HVHF-drilling. (Chapter 5)

The Town of Colden—and perhaps hundreds of other small New York towns—are unable, or unwilling, to govern in accord with basic democratic principles.

The town's one-branch government structure—especially the absence of a functioning executive branch—set the stage for a policy making process best described as muddling-through. And with the general lack of top-down leadership, the HVHF-drilling debate was effectively delegated to the poorly trained, and apparently pro-HVHF-drilling advisors manning the town's planning board.

The predictable happened: In the end, the voice of active, informed citizens calling on their elected officials to protect them from the health and safety risks associated with HVHF-drilling was outmatched by a government lacking democratic governance.

Why is this not a surprise? Way back in the 1950s and 1960s, studies of small town governments (See Appendix D) identified many of the same governing weaknesses exhibited by officials in the Town of Colden during the HVHF-drilling debate. Little has changed. Too many small towns still lack professional administrators and standard public personnel management practices. Small towns are still mainly run by part-time, untrained, amateur administrators operating in an organizational structure that tends to concentrate power in the hands of a few members of the community.

State lawmakers are partly responsible for the governing crisis in New York's small towns. They have known for a long time that it is folly to count on small town officials to voluntarily increase their administrative competence without state-ordered mandates to do so.

State legislators increased the public powers of small town officials, including, land use control powers, without, at the same time, making sure the officials exercising these powers were competent to carry out their increasingly complex duties. Even as studies documented the amateurish quality of town planning boards, state lawmakers in Albany continued to pass timid legislative fixes, apparently believing in a myth—that local, small town officials, with little public administration expertise and experience, would somehow improve their administrative competence by imposing on themselves effective training programs and administrative practices.

State lawmakers have the power and responsibility to raise the competence of small town governments to better serve their citizens by imposing and enforcing administrative standards, including the requirement that all towns employ (at least on a part-time basis) a trained public administrator responsible for the conduct of the town's business in accord with democratic principles of government. But how likely is it that New York State lawmakers will do so?

In his 2006 book, *Three Men in a Room: The Inside Story of Power and Betrayal in an American Statehouse*, the five term member of the New York State Senate, Seymour P. Lachman, describes a legislative process unlikely to seriously challenge local governments in need of reform. Three men, the governor, the speaker of the assembly and the majority leader of the state senate, control the fate of any attempt to bring about local government reforms.

While there are 212 elected members of the legislature in Albany, Lachman tells us, "Should a member of one of the two houses author a piece of legislation, the leader decides which committee it goes to, whether it is passed in the committee, and when or even if it gets passed out for a (predetermined) vote on the floor. The leader of each house can stop a bill from advancing at virtually any point in its journey toward becoming law. This power is accepted and acceded to by most legislators, who realize they can probably remain in office comfortably as long as they don't challenge the system."

In his 2017 book, *Failed State: Dysfunction and Corruption in an American Statehouse,* Lachman confirms that little has changed. The chances are not good that a group of locally elected members of the state legislature, or even the New York State Legislative Commission on Rural Resources, can muster enough political momentum to bring the governing process in small New York towns into the 21st century.

It is, of course, risky to apply the findings of a single case study to other towns in New York State. But, if the Town of Colden represents a fair picture of the governing process found in other small New York towns, it is the responsibility of both state legislators, and of officials in small New York towns, to carefully consider whether the following options could improve governance in small New York towns.

It is time to stop pretending small towns are capable of, ipso facto, performing the administrative duties traditionally a part of democratic governance in America. In small New York towns, part-time, amateur administrators may not even be aware of the full scope of the duties required by democratic governance, let alone how to deliver them.

It is time to consider radical changes. For example, simply disbanding a town's dysfunctional planning board might very well improve the quality of land use planning. Instead of turning to their ill-prepared local planning boards when making land use decisions, town board members would then be more likely to seek professional planning advice from available public and private organizations.

What follows are options aimed at improving the policy-making process in small towns. The goal is to shift policy making responsibilities from part-time, undertrained, small town officials, to larger, (consolidated) town units, or to county governments, staffed with trained executive branch officials capable of managing public affairs in accord with the principles of democratic public administration.

These options are offered as a starting point for consideration by citizens, town officials and state and local legislators. Each option will certainly raise many what-if questions and objections from defenders of the status-quo.

Options for Change

Option #1. Merge towns with a population under 4,000 into county governments. Shift all tasks, both routine service tasks and more demanding policy management duties, to the appropriate county government. Town highway departments and equipment, operating within existing town boundaries, would become subunits of the county government.

The organization of all but eight of New York's 57 counties outside of New York City, include an executive branch headed by an elected executive or an appointed manager or administrator.

Some county governments, especially rural counties, may need staffing increases in order to assume added responsibilities. But, with the elimination of current town administrative and operating costs, funds should be available to do so.

Option #2. Consolidate a number of adjacent towns into a single unit of town government with a population of at least 20,000. Create an independent executive branch in the larger town unit headed by a trained town manager (or, alternatively, a part-time circuit-riding town manager) responsible for conducting the town's affairs in accordance with the principles of American public administration.

Under this option, the work load of the town board will be limited to the duties of an oversight, law-making, body. The town manager will be responsible for the day-to-day operation of the town government.

For example, the merger of five towns in southern Erie County—the towns of Wales, Holland, Sardinia, Colden and Concord—would provide a single, consolidated town with a population of more than 20,000 people. Since this option eliminates twenty paid town board positions, these savings could provide a large share of the town manager's salary.

Option # 3. An option currently popular with conservatives and Republicans seeking to limit the scope of government, is to privatize routine community services, such as road work and trash collection in small towns and transfer all governmental services to the county.

This is an attractive option since officials in many small towns are not equipped to handle complex public policy decisions, and the performance of routine community services, such as road work and trash collection, can easily be handled by a non-government entity.

One way this might play-out is: Incorporate each former small town as a private home owners association with its primary duties being highway maintenance and trash collection.

All town-level government duties—issuing licenses, passport services, tax collection, etc.—would be transferred to the county. The homeowners association would be funded by annual membership dues collected from each member.

AFTERWORD

What is the long-term prospect for democracy in America? An unstated assumption throughout this study—and a view widely accepted by most political scientists—is that liberal democracy, especially in America, will remain our only legitimate political regime, that democracy is here to stay. But is that the case?

In the July 2016 issue of *Journal of Democracy,* an article titled, "The Danger of Deconsolidation," by Roberto Stefan Fao, Yascha Mounk, and Ronald F. Inglehart, looks at the changing beliefs of citizens living in a number of supposedly "consolidated democracies" around the world, including the United States.

They found that Americans have "become more cynical about the value of democracy as a political system, less hopeful that anything they do might influence public policy, and more willing to express support for authoritarian alternatives."

The authors, using World Values Surveys data identify the following trends among American citizens.

(1.) 2014: To the question, "Is it essential to live in a country that is governed democratically?" 72% of the American respondents born in the 1930s said "Yes;" 50% of the respondents born in the 1960s said "Yes;" but only 30% of the respondents born in the 1980s said "Yes."

(2.) 2011: To the statement, "Having a Democratic Political System is a bad or very bad way to run a country," 12% of the respondents 65 years of age and older agreed; 17% of the respondents 35-44 years of age agreed; 22% of the respondents 25-34 years of age agreed; but 24% of the American respondents 16-24 years of age agreed that a democratic system of government is a bad idea.

(3.) To the statement, "Do you think that it would be a good, or very good, thing for the army to rule?" In 1995 one in sixteen (6%) American respondents agreed, but in 2016 one in six (16%) Americans agreed that army rule is a good idea.

(4.) In the United States, the share of citizens who believe that it would be better to have a strong leader who does not have to bother with parliament and elections is on the rise. In 1995 24% of the American respondents held this view, but by 2011 that figure had increased to 32%.

The authors conclude:

"The degree to which a democracy is consolidated depends on three key characteristics: the degree of popular support for democracy as a system of government; the degree to which anti-system parties and movements are weak or nonexistent; and the degree to which the democratic rules are accepted...democracy may one day cease to be the 'only game in town': Citizens who once accepted democracy as the only legitimate form of government could become more open to authoritarians alternatives."

* * * * *

Few Americans would: seek advice from a health clinic run by untrained doctors and nurses; attend a school run by untrained teachers; or take their dog to an untrained vet. Why then do so many Americans living in small towns tolerate local governments run by untrained public officials?

Maybe, just maybe, little by little, Americans sense that

fundamental principles of democratic governance are no longer guiding the actions of public officials. Maybe that is why so
many Americans say: living in a democracy is not essential; that
a democratic system of government is a bad way to run a country; and that army rule is a good thing.

APPENDIX A

Town of Colden, New York: A Profile

Town governments in New York State are overwhelmingly small and rural. In 2010, sixty percent, or 562 towns, had populations less than 4,000. With a population of 3,265, the Town of Colden, size-wise, is more or less typical of a majority of New York towns.

The 36.5 square mile Town of Colden, New York, located 12 miles south of Buffalo, is statistically a part of the Erie County/Niagara County metropolitan region with a combined 2010 population of 1,135,509. The Town of Colden is located on the outer fringe of this large metropolitan region.

Population. Historically, the populations of the City of Buffalo and the Town of Colden have gone up and down. Between 1860 and 1930 Colden's population slowly declined from 1,568 to 1,217. Then its population took off, more than doubling from 1,528 in 1940 to 3,128 in 1980 largely, I suspect, in response to the post-war growth of American suburbs. Since 1980 Colden's population has stabilized with only slight changes thereafter and, in the 2010 census, the town was home to 3,265 residents, 98.6% of whom were white.

During this period, the City of Buffalo's population fell by about 61% from 580,132 in 1950 to 357,870 in 1980.

Economy. In the distant past dairy farms may have played a significant role in the town's economy. Gentlemen farmers still graze a few cattle, sheep or horses here and there, but nothing on a commercial scale. However, hay fields are still a common land use.

While there are no large manufacturing or service employers in the town, the Town of Colden does contain a golf course, a 56 acre recreational vehicle park and is next door to the Kissing Bridge ski complex. About 90% of the town's residents commute to work with a 32-minute, mean travel time by car truck or van.

The top occupations reported by the town's employed adults are: construction, 12.6%; manufacturing, 9.4%; public administration, 10.6%; educational, health or social services and professional, 26.1%; and scientific and waste management services 10.1%.

Graphs and charts comparing economic factors for the Town of Colden with surrounding towns can be found at: http://www.towncharts.com/New-York/Economy/Colden-town-NY-Economy-data.html

Public Employment. The following map compares the Town of Colden's population and its public employment numbers with other towns in Erie County. Two trends are evident. First, the more populated towns, and those with the larger number of full-time employees, are located in the northern part of the county. Here the Town of Amherst, for example, home to 122,366 persons, employs more than 600 full-time workers.

Second, not only are the towns in the southern part of the county more rural and sparsely populated, there is a clustering of four small towns, with populations less than 4,000 in the county's southeast corner. Here we find the towns of Wales, Holland, Sardinia and Colden.

Towns in Erie County, New York 2015

LEGEND: Population/Full-time Employees/Part-time Employees

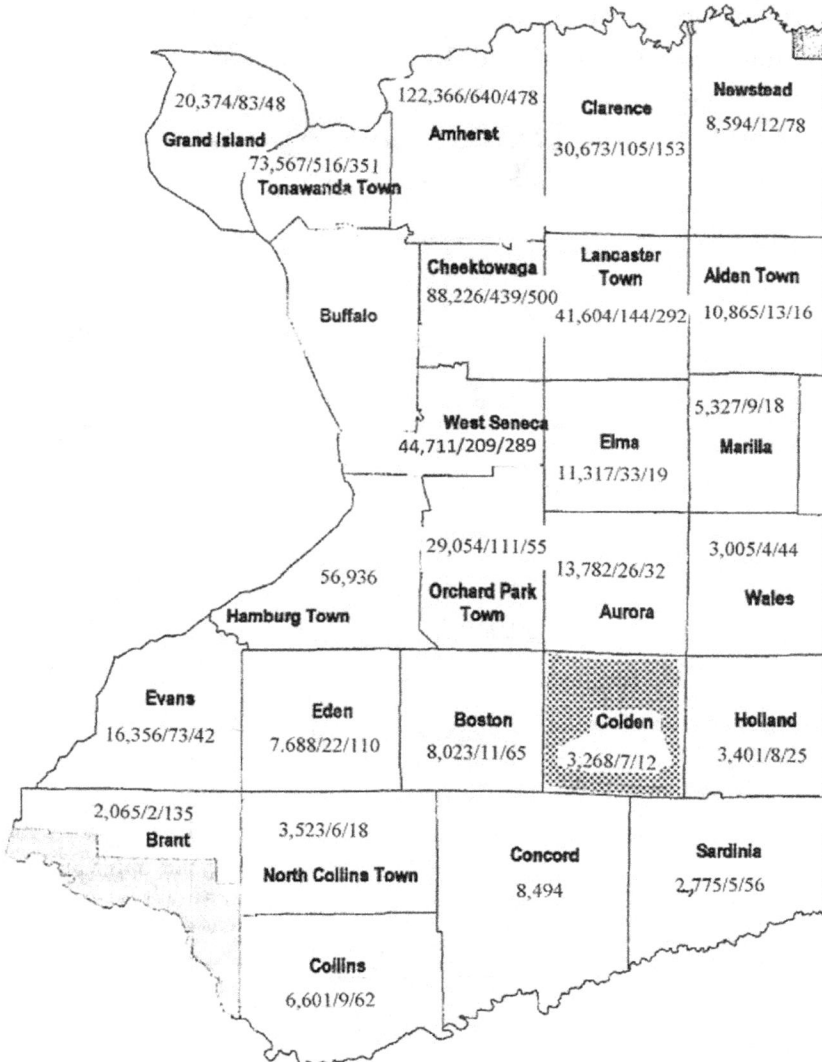

Town	Data
Grand Island	20,374/83/48
Amherst	122,366/640/478
Clarence	30,673/105/153
Newstead	8,594/12/78
Tonawanda Town	73,567/516/351
Cheektowaga	88,226/439/500
Lancaster Town	41,604/144/292
Alden Town	10,865/13/16
West Seneca	44,711/209/289
Elma	11,317/33/19
Marilla	5,327/9/18
Orchard Park Town	29,054/111/55
Aurora	13,782/26/32
Wales	3,005/4/44
Hamburg Town	56,936
Evans	16,356/73/42
Eden	7.688/22/110
Boston	8,023/11/65
Colden	3,268/7/12
Holland	3,401/8/25
Brant	2,065/2/135
North Collins Town	3,523/6/18
Concord	8,494
Sardinia	2,775/5/56
Collins	6,601/9/62

Source: NYS Comptroller's Office

For another perspective, the following diagram compares the fulltime employment of selected municipalities and New York State. Erie County's large number of fulltime workers, (more than

4,000) compared to the seven fulltime employees (four of whom are assigned to the town's highway department) in the Town of Colden, suggest that the county supplies the town with a rather robust level of public services, including law enforcement and maintenance of county roads located in the town.

Town of Colden in Perspective

Full-time Employees 2016

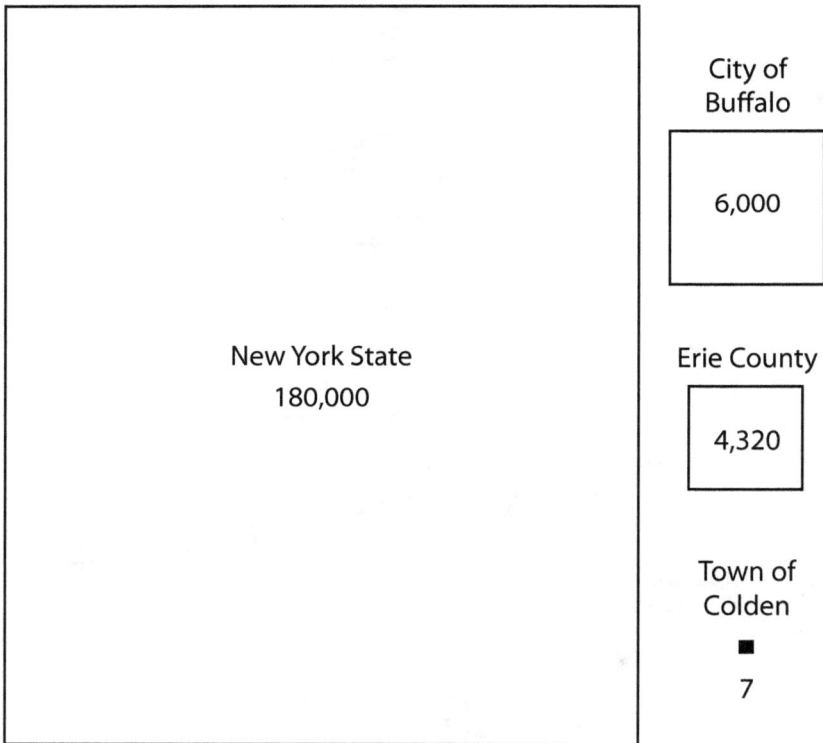

	City of Buffalo
	6,000

New York State 180,000	Erie County
	4,320

Town of Colden

■

7

<u>Town Expenditures</u>. The following table, based on fiscal year 2016 data from the New York State Comptroller's Office, provides a snapshot of what it takes to finance the Town of Colden for one year.

Table I

TOWN OF COLDEN: 2016 EXPENDITURES

Category	Expenditure	Percent
Transportation	$ 677,564	38.4
General Government	$ 332,385	18.8
Employee Benefits	$ 254,803	14.4
Sanitation/Trash	$ 211,607	12.0
Debt Service	$ 94,154	5.3
Culture & Recreation	$ 72,805	4.1
Utilities	$ 90,676	5.1
Public Safety	$ 26,261	1.4
Community Services	$ 2,900	0.0016
Other	$ 1,570	0.0008
TOTAL	$1,764,727	99.5

Far and away, maintenance of town roads is the most costly public service provided by the Town of Colden. And more than one-half of the town's total expenditures go for just two service categories: transportation and trash collection. Add in employee benefits and we are approaching two-thirds of the total budget.

APPENDIX B

Colden Well Being Survey Instrument

EDDM RETAIL
PAID
U.S. POSTAGE
ECRWSS
PRSRT STD

Local
Postal Customer

Colden Well Being
PO Box 53, Colden, NY 14033

Colden Well Being

WHAT DO YOU WANT THE FUTURE OF COLDEN TO LOOK LIKE?

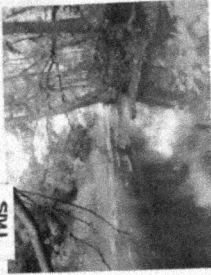

This

Or this?

It's time to decide what's truly important to you and your loved ones.

It's time to decide the future of Colden.

Colden Well Being

THE TIME TO ACT IS NOW

Colden is not the only town in New York that has concerns regarding the potential adverse impacts from fracking. Presently, 180 local communities in NY have adopted bans or moratoriums on the practice of fracking within their community and many more are taking the steps necessary toward a ban or moratorium.

If you care about the quality of life here in Colden, you must speak out now and support legislation to ban fracking within the boundaries of our town.

JOIN IN OUR EFFORT BY SIGNING AND RETURNING THE ATTACHED RESPONSE CARD TODAY:

Colden Well Being
PO Box 53, Colden, NY 14033

For additional information on the effects of fracking on our community, to support our activities, or to join us at our meetings, visit us at facebook.com/ColdenWellBeing or email us at coldenwellbeing@gmail.com.

Join us at Town Board meetings to help let Town Board members know you don't want to see Colden turned into an industrial zone.

⚠ PLEASE ACT NOW BECAUSE ONCE YOU FRACK, YOU CAN'T TURN BACK!

[QR code]

Facebook.com/ ColdenWellBeing

Colden Well Being is a group of Colden citizens dedicated to protecting our water rights against the threat of hydraulic fracturing.

This mailer paid for by donations from Colden residents.

THE FUTURE OF OUR COMMUNITY

"Each landowner within the community is at the mercy of his neighbors, and all must cooperate in the common interest if they are to enjoy maximum benefit of the Town and its residents." —Master Plan Town of Colden

THEIR CLAIMS

Industry supporters claim that fracking will create jobs and boost the local economy. The truth is that the work is performed mainly by transient, out-of-state workers already employed by the drilling companies who leave town when the work is done. If there are any local benefits, they are temporary, which is why analysts call fracking a "boom and bust" industry.

The financial benefits from fracking will be concentrated in the hands of a few large landowners. However, everyone in the community will have to live with the potential consequences of this decision as the social, environmental, and health impacts associated with fracking will not be contained behind someone's property line.

Presently, the industry is exempt from most major federal regulations enacted to protect public health and the environment. Only the state has the authority to regulate the industry.

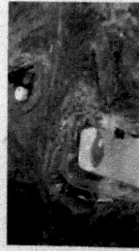

The pictured landscape will be/and after drilling activities in Colden has past survey.

✋ Local control extends only to banning fracking within the community or allowing it.

IT'S ABOUT OUR QUALITY OF LIFE

The many things that define our quality of life here in Colden—**fresh air and clean water, beautiful views, a peaceful environment, quiet streets**—are all at risk from the dangers posed by the process of high-volume hydraulic fracturing or "fracking".

The picturesque and natural setting in Colden is important to our families' quality of life and is worth preserving.

Fracking is a method used to extract natural gas and raises new, potentially significant adverse impacts to human health and the environment. To extract the gas trapped in tight rock formations like the Marcellus and Utica Shale, millions of gallons of water, sand, and potentially toxic chemicals are injected into a deep, horizontal well to break open or "fracture" the surrounding rock.

Recovered fracking fluid may contain naturally-occurring **radioactive materials and formerly buried heavy metals.** The millions of gallons of fracking fluid that do not resurface pose a long-term threat to drinking water supplies. Repeated fracking of wells further pushes the fluids out and threatens larger areas.

Known human carcinogens including **benzene and toluene** are just a few of the over 600 chemicals identified so far for use in the hydraulic fracturing process.

WHAT CAN YOU EXPECT FROM FRACKING?
OUR CONCERNS:

Water Contamination & Depletion

One of the greatest risks posed by fracking is the threat to our water. The majority of our town relies on private wells. The industrial activity associated with fracking operations can contaminate water supplies through accidents, well-casing failures, construction activity, runoff, and spills. Uncovered fracking chemicals and methane migration remain long-term threats to groundwater. **Millions of gallons of fresh water are used during each frack process**—water that is lost forever for use as drinking water for humans and animals, for agriculture and other uses. Depletion of this **precious and limited resource** is a fear even the industry acknowledges.

Even during this past summer's drought, National Fuel admitted to withdrawing up to 120,000 gallons of fresh water from local streams.

Air Pollution

Large scale fracking operations require the use of a significantly greater number of trucks and equipment than the conventional drilling of individual vertical gas wells. Air emissions from fracking sites will have an impact on the surrounding air quality with the potential to harm the **respiratory and neurological health** of nearby residents, domestic animals, and wildlife, as already observed at current fracking sites.

Increased Traffic and Noise

In addition to millions of gallons of water, trucks supporting fracking operations transport tons of equipment, huge amounts of chemicals, and enormous quantities of fracking waste. **The development of each new well could require 3400 truck trips.** This level of traffic has the potential to result in significant adverse impacts on our roads... **increasing repair and maintenance costs which will be borne by taxpayers**...and presents serious safety concerns as truck drivers try to negotiate our roads. Nearby residents would be subjected to noise around the clock during drilling operations as well as from compressors, etc., that process retrieved gas into the distribution network.

Loss of Views and Aesthetics

The construction of new roads, multi-acre well sites (**as many as one site every square mile**), possible compressor stations, and new pipelines involve a significant amount of land clearing and excavation of previously undeveloped and verdant land, marring the natural landscape. Heavy industrial fracking operations would severely impact the quiet, rural character of our community.

Declining Property Values

Our homes represent **our most valuable asset.** Many banks and insurance companies consider gas-leased properties to be unacceptable risks and are denying mortgages, loans, and insurance coverage.

New York's compulsory integration law can force neighbors who never signed leases into drilling pools, allowing frackers to drill under their properties without leases. Property values decline not only for those who have signed leases, but for everyone in the surrounding area.

APPENDIX C

Town of Colden Survey Instrument

Attention Colden Town Resident

High Volume Hydraulic Fracturing – Is this something you support or is this something you would not support in the Town of Colden?

As your Supervisor and Town Board Members prepare to address the issue of **High Volume Hydraulic Fracturing** within the town limits, we want to give town residents the chance to have their voices heard.

Your Supervisor and Town Board Members urge you, if you haven't already, to research this practice so you can make an educated decision on the practice of **High Volume Hydraulic Fracturing.**

As your elected Supervisor of Colden I am asking for your input by filling this mailing out and sending it back to the town hall at **S-8812 State Road PO Box 335 Colden, NY 14033,** directed to the Supervisor's office. This mailing has to be received **no later than October 7, 2014.**

Name: _____

Address: _____

_____

Phone#: _____

_____ I **am in Favor** of High Volume Hydraulic Fracturing in the Town

of Colden.

_____ I **am not in Favor** of High Volume Hydraulic Fracturing in the

Town of Colden.

Comments may be added to the back of this mailing. Please include your name, address and phone number above.

Thank you for your time and remember your voice does matter!!!

88

APPENDIX D

Small Town Governance —Then & Now

To put this recent snapshot of the Town of Colden into an historical perspective, we need to go back in time and draw on the work of two respected public management scholars writing in the 1950-1960s, and put their descriptions of small town government 60 years ago into a THEN and NOW format.

Citing short passages (the THEN) from each scholar's book, and assuming they fairly reflected the status of small New York towns 60 years ago, a companion NOW description is added, based on the findings of this study.

Roscoe Martin, *Grass Roots: Rural Democracy in America*

As municipalities in the late nineteenth century grew larger and the public services they delivered became more complex, public agencies adopted more effective management practices including relying on a more professional workforce. But, as pointed out in Syracuse University professor Roscoe Martin's 1957 book, *Grass Roots: Rural Democracy in America*, public administration in small towns did not kept pace with the administrative advances adopted in larger municipalities.

Martin acknowledges that little governments are in "harmony with the American heritage of agrarian democracy," still, he challenges the proposition, "that local government, and especially rural local government, is desirable and therefore in all important respects good."

* * * * *

THEN. "When the chores of government are discharged by friends and neighbors, the citizen feels that he 'belongs'…that he can chat things over with them on the doorstep in the evening."

NOW. Yes and no. Many citizens in the Town of Colden do feel a certain civic intimacy living in a small town where one's neighbors are in charge. But, once the town's daily routine is upset, when a decision must be made on a controversial, risk-filled public issue, such as HVHF-drilling in the town, Colden's officials were not so eager to chat things over.

* * * * *

THEN. "Grass-roots government is held to be direct, personal, intimate, informal, face-to-face...there is a minimum of paperwork and of record-keeping, for democracy is not a thing to be written down but only to be experienced...big government is held to represent the opposite of almost everything that little government stands for..."

NOW. Officials in the Town of Colden, unlike in larger municipalities, shortcut standard personnel management practices, such as, not bothering to prepare annual written performance evaluations (paperwork) for their workforce.

This aversion to personnel management and training is evident elsewhere. The chaotic condition of the planning board's training program perhaps reflects a reluctance for town officials to initiate and impose a well-designed training course—and one requiring a bit of hard work—upon friends appointed to the town's planning board.

* * * * *

THEN. "Rural government is almost wholly amateur. It is amateur in two senses. First, there are few of the tools of professional management now widely in use among the larger units... Little government is amateur in the further sense that it is personal, not professional."

NOW. This is still a valid general description of public administration in the Town of Colden.

*   *   *   *   *

THEN. "Grass-roots politics frequently involves little public policy; on the contrary, it may be largely of a personal character; and it may indeed be cast in terms of personal loyalty rather than in those terms usually held appropriate to the public arena."

NOW. Still is the case. The HVHF-drilling debate in the Town of Colden exposed an utter inability of town officials to put together a decision making process capable of producing a rational HVHF-drilling policy for the town.

*   *   *   *   *

THEN. "The student of public affairs distinguishes broadly between government, politics and administration; but in little governments these distinctions are not valid, or if valid in principle, are not overtly useful in practice...one of the prime problems of public administration is to develop managers with a general sense of government and administration...the lines separating politics from government and both from administration blur and grow dim, with the result that nothing more than a general impression of government remains."

NOW. Still an accurate description of public administration in the Town of Colden, as amply demonstrated by the behavior of town board members and planning board members during the HVHF-drilling debate.

*   *   *   *   *

THEN. "The assumption is that the citizen learns about democracy from participation in the affairs of local government.

But what does he learn and how does he learn it? What is the curriculum offered? Who are the faculty? What are the teaching and learning materials?"

NOW. If these key questions had been carefully addressed by Colden officials, they might have produced an effective training program for the town's planning board—but the questions were never asked.

* * * * *

THEN. "Government at the grass roots is particularly impervious to change. If the capacity to respond to changing conditions is an attribute of a vital democracy, then it may be argued that grass roots government is less democratic than that of either the nation or the state."

NOW. The Town of Colden has successfully avoided adopting the three-branch form of government, and with it, separation-of-power safeguards most Americans enjoy. The state has given the town the authority to create an independent executive branch, but the Town of Colden officials prefer concentration of power in a few hands and the absence of accountability checks on their actions.

In addition, officials in the Town of Colden, and perhaps many other small New York towns, have avoided adopting prudent management practices, such as the efforts of the state legislature to initiate effective training of planning board members.

* * * * *

Morton Grodzins, *The American System (1966)*

Grodzins, at the time a professor at the University of Chicago, targets the effects of political and social atmospheres in small towns on the administrative process.

THEN. "In small communities homogeneity of outlook is

combined with inequality of power. A small group of farmers or businessmen, a single politician, or a rich family of old settlers can frequently control the entire politics of a rural community… [and]…represents an effective monopolization of power over those things which the rural government does and refuses to do.

"The small size of the community means that dissenters find difficulty in organizing opposition, a difficulty that is compounded because of the wide range of personal, social and economic penalties that may be exacted by the ruling group…possibilities of clique and one-man rule are maximized, ideal images of small town democracy notwithstanding."

NOW. Monopolization of power was on display in the Town of Colden during the HV HF-drilling debate. After two years of debate in which the town's own Hydrofracking Committee, the town's own Environmental Board and two surveys of the town's population all called for banning HVHF-drilling in Colden, the town supervisor, when confronted with the town's lack of enforcement of its own ethical standard, summarily ended the town's attempt to enact a HVHF-drilling ban. No checks on his power. No justification given to the people for his actions. No accountability to the citizens for leaving the town's citizens exposed to health and safety risks linked to HVHF-drilling.

APPENDIX E

Planning Board Training Records

In March 2015, a Freedom of Information Request was filed with the Colden Town Clerk, that read: "I hereby make application to examine the following records: For the last five years (2010-2014) the records describing the annual training received by Town of Colden planning board members."

The town's response:

Member #1: 2013 only, workshop with town lawyer; video conference, Clemson School of Agriculture and Forestry; agricultural district training by Erie County Department of Planning & Environment.

Member #2: 2013 only, planning and zoning training from Jaeckle, Fleischmann & Mugel.

Member #3: 2010 only, confronting NIMBYs, presented by the Erie County Department of Planning & Environment.

Member #4: 2010, confronting NIMBYs, presented by the Erie County Department of Planning & Environment; 2013, farmland protection presented by the Orleans County Department of Planning and Development; 2013, planning and zoning training from Jaeckle, Fleischmann & Mugel; 2014 planning and zoning training from Jaeckle, Fleischmann & Mugel; 2014, SEQRA Training presented by the Genesee County & Wyoming County.

Member #5: 2008, SEQRA and site plan review, presented by TVGA Consultants; 2008, Farmland protection/right to farm, mining permits, presented by TVGA Consultants; 2013, 8-hour local government planning workshop presented by the Genesee/Finger Lakes Regional Planning Council; 2014, 5.5-hour local government planning workshop presented by the Genesee/

Finger Lakes Regional Planning Council; 2014, 8-hours of citizen planner training presented by the University at Buffalo Architecture and Planning department.

Member #6: No training records provided.

Member #7: No training records provided.

Planning Board Personnel Records

In June 2016, a Freedom of Information Request was filed with the Colden Town Clerk, that read,

"I hereby make application to examine the following records: In filling past vacancies on its planning board and environmental board, the Town of Colden has mailed to each town household a candidates solicitation notice announcing vacancies and including the requirements that applicants submit to the town clerk a letter of interest and a resume for review by the town board.

"It is requested that I be provided copies of the letters of interest and resumes received by the town clerk from all current members of the planning board."

The town's response:

o The letter of interest and resume for only two of the seven current planning board members was received; and

o For the other five planning board members, only the letter of interest—without a resume.

It is unclear why the Town of Colden asks planning board candidates for their resumes. In other municipalities resumes are used to evaluate and compare the planning board candidate's skills against the skills listed in a formal, agency-prepared job, or position, description.

But, since the Town of Colden has not prepared a job or position description for the position of planning board appointee, the missing five resumes are not, apparently, a big deal. What is the administrative value of a resume in the absence of town-prepared planning board skill standards?

For that matter, in the absence of a planning board job or position description identifying the skills needed by planning board members to perform their duties, how can the town prepare meaningful courses of instruction targeting non-identified skills?

APPENDIX F

Filing of a Misdemeanor Complaint with Town Court,
Town of Colden, NY

December 1, 2014

(To avoid a conflict of interest, the case was transferred
to the Town of Boston)

Preliminary Information

This accusatory instrument, a Misdemeanor Complaint for offenses allegedly committed in the Town of Colden, NY, is hereby filed by the complainant, a person with knowledge of the offenses charged (New York Criminal Procedure Law, Section 100.15) in the local criminal court located in the Town of Colden, the independent, judicial branch of the town government with jurisdiction over all offenses other than felonies (New York Criminal Procedure Law, Section 10).

Two supporting depositions are filed with this accusatory instrument.

Two attachments are also filed with this accusatory instrument.

Accusatory Information

The Town of Colden Planning Board chairman is hereby accused of Official Misconduct, a misdemeanor offense under the New York Penal Law, Title L, Offenses Against Public Administration, Article 195.

Following the chairman's receipt of the Colden Supervisor's

May 13, 2013 memo (Attachment 1) requesting an advisory report from the Planning Board, the chairman, with the intent to deny citizens of the Town of Colden, NY, the benefits inherent in a local government administered according to the rule of law and due process contained in the town's locally adopted laws, knowingly refrained from performing duties imposed upon him by Colden Town law, as follows:

COUNT ONE

The chairman failed to perform the duties imposed upon him by the Town of Colden local law, Chapter 11, Ethics, Section 11.4.E, which reads:

"Disclosure of interest in legislation. To the extent that he knows thereof, a member of the Town Board and any officer or employee of the Town of Colden, whether paid or unpaid, who participates in the discussion or gives official opinion to the Town Board or any other official board or agency on any legislation before the Town Board or any other official board or agency shall publicly disclose on the official record the nature and extent of any direct or indirect financial or other private interest he has in such legislation."

COUNT TWO

The chairman failed to perform the duties imposed upon him by the Town of Colden local law Chapter 108, Zoning, Article XXV, 108-130 B. which reads:

"Referral to Planning Board. Each proposed amendment, except those initiated by the Town Planning Board, shall be referred to the Town Planning Board for an advisory report prior to the public hearing held by the Town Board. In reporting, the Town Planning Board shall fully state its reasons for recommending or opposing the adoption of such proposed amendment and, if it shall recommend adoption, shall describe any changes in conditions which it believes make the amendment desirable and shall state whether such amendment is in harmony with a master or comprehensive plan for land use in the town."

Factual Information
GAS DRILLING MORATORIUM

In April 2012, the Town of Colden passed the first of two local laws, each establishing a six-month moratorium on the use of land for high volume hydraulic fracturing gas and oil drilling. In April 2013 and then again in March, 2014, the original moratorium statute was extended for one additional year. Each law stated, in part, that:

"The Town Board finds that the commercial extraction of natural gas and oil by hydraulic fracturing or horizontal gas well drilling in the rural environment of the Town of Colden may violate the rights of residents and impose a significant threat to their health, safety and welfare [and] the activity may pose a threat to some, if not all, of the natural water supply upon which the Town of Colden relies as its sole source of water."

HYDROFRACKING COMMITTEE

On August 27, 2012 the Colden Town Board established the Hydrofracking Committee to "Compile a list of zoning concerns to be incorporated into our zoning ordinances."

On April 12, 2013, the Hydrofracking Committee sent its report, *Gas Drilling in the Town of Colden, A Report to the Colden Town Board and All Colden Citizens*, to the Town Board recommending that the town's zoning ordinance be amended to prohibit High Volume Hydraulic Fracturing drilling for gas and oil in Colden.

COUNT ONE

A review of the Town of Colden records maintained by the Town Clerk, shows that as of September 15, 2014, more than sixteen months after receiving the Hydrofracking Committee's gas drilling report for his review, the Planning Board chairman continues to violate Chapter 11, Ethics, Section 11.4.E of the Town of Colden laws by not requiring members of the Planning Board, himself included, to publicly disclose, on the official record, the nature and extent of any direct or indirect financial or other private interest planning board members have in the oil and gas industry.

The chairman's continuing violation of Chapter 11, Ethics, Section 11.4.E, has denied the citizens of Colden the basic American benefits of rule by law, legally mandated administrative due process in the conduct of public affairs by Town of Colden officials and has also denied the citizens of the Town of Colden their right to know whether their appointed Planning Board officials are acting in the interest of the community or acting to promote their own private interests in the oil and gas industry.

Members of the town's official Hydrofracking Committee have filed public oil and gas disclosure statements with the Colden Town Clerk in compliance with Chapter 11, Ethics, Section 11.4.E. Members of the town's Environmental Board also filed public oil and gas disclosure statements with the Colden Town Clerk in compliance with Chapter 11, Ethics, Section 11.4.E prior to sending the Environmental Board's advisory report to the Town Board approving the proposed zoning amendment recommended in the Hydrofracking Committee report.

In addition, Chapter 11, Ethics, Section 11.7, titled "Disciplinary Action," reads: "Any violation of the provisions of this Code of Ethics shall constitute cause for suspension or removal from office or employment or such other disciplinary action as the Town Board may consider advisable, after a hearing, in the manner provided by law..." To date, the Colden Town Board has, to my knowledge, taken no action to carry out its legal duties to enforce the provisions of Colden Local Law, Chapter 11, Ethics, Section 11.4.E.

Chapter 28-3.B of the Colden town law also states that the duties assigned to the town's Enforcement Officer, include to "enforce all rules, regulations, ordinances and local laws of the Town of Colden." To date, the Colden Code Enforcement Officer has, to my knowledge, taken no action to enforce the disclosure requirements of Colden Local Law, Chapter 11, Ethics, Section 11.4.E.

COUNT TWO

On May 13, 2013, the Colden Town Board requested that the Planning Board review the Hydrofracking Committee report. The Town Supervisor's request stated, "The Town Board would like to see the Planning Board prepare recommendations for a zoning ordinance as it pertains to high volume hydraulic fracturing and the Town of Colden's Master Plans..."

To this date, more than sixteen months later, the chairman has failed to comply with the official duties Town of Colden local law Chapter 108, Zoning, Article XXV, 108-130 B imposes on him, including the necessary steps a Planning Board must take to properly prepare the legally required advisory report.

The Planning Board has not held public gatherings to discuss the Hydrofracking Committee report and its recommendation to prohibit high volume hydraulic fracturing for gas and oil in the Town of Colden. The Planning Board has not provided the Town Board or the public with reports describing its research on relevant oil and gas drilling issues. The Planning Board has not taken the required action to evaluate whether or not the proposed zoning ordinance is in harmony with the values and policies contained in the Town's master Land use plan, *Master Plan 2002, Town of Colden, NY*.

The chairman's continuing violation of Chapter 108, Zoning, Article XXV, 108-130 B, has denied the citizens of Colden the basic American benefits of rule by law and legal administrative due process, as specified in the Town of Colden local law.

Chapter 28-3.B of the Colden town law also states that the duties assigned to the town's Enforcement Officer, include to "enforce all rules, regulations, ordinances and local laws of the Town of Colden." To date, the Town of Colden Code Enforcement Officer, has not acted to enforce the provisions of Colden Local Law, Chapter 108-130 B.

* * * * *

Attachments:
1. May 13, 2013 Memo from Colden Supervisor to Planning Board Chairman

MEMO

From: Town of Colden Supervisor's Office
To: Town of Colden Planning Board Chairman
Date: 5/13/13
Ref: Gas Drilling

Confirming our conversation, the Colden Town Board requests that the Planning Board review the Gas Drilling in the Town of Colden report prepared by the Hydrofracking Committee.

The Town Board would like to see the Planning Board prepare recommendations for a zoning ordinance as it pertains to HVHF and the Town of Colden's Master Plans adopted in 1970, 1993 and 2002.

Following your research, the Town Board would like to see the Planning Board, Environmental Board and Hydrofracking Committee meet and work together to finalize and detail a recommendation to the Town Board.

Respectfully,
Colden Town Supervisor

* * * * *

November 30, 2015

To: Presiding Justice, Town of Boston Court
From: Complainant
Subject: Response to Defendant's November 2, 2015
Motion to Dismiss

The subject Motion to Dismiss, submitted by Defense Counsel, contains a number of serious misleading and factual errors. The purpose of this communication is to bring these questionable passages to your attention as you weigh whether or not to proceed with this case.

In order to concentrate the court's attention on Count Two, the central component of this complaint, I hereby request that Count One be withdrawn.

* * * * *

Count Two in the Motion to Dismiss hinges on the court's acceptance of two flawed premises:

(1.) That Town of Colden local law Chapter 108, Zoning, Article XXV, 108-130 B applies only to the final, written draft language, stage of the zoning ordinance amendment process: and,

(2.) That the Town's Hydrofracking Committee report, including a recommendation to amend the Town's zoning ordinance to prohibit high volume hydraulic fracturing (HVHF) for oil and gas, was never properly referred to the Town Planning Board for review, per Town Law 271(14).

* * * * *

Count Two

Paragraphs 10 to 13 in the subject Notice of Motion to Dismiss pertain to Count Two. They are as follows, with my response to each.

Paragraph 10. "The complaint does not state any factual information to support the allegation that any proposed amendment to the Town of Colden Zoning Code regarding hydrofracking was referred to the Planning Board for an advisory report."

Response. In fact, the Town of Colden Supervisor's May 13, 2013 Memo to the Planning Board chairman (Attachment 1 to the complaint) officially referred to the Planning Board the Hydrofracking Committee report, *Gas Drilling in the Town of Colden,* dated April 11, 2013— containing the recommendation that the Town prepare an amendment to the town's zoning code to prohibit high volume, hydraulic fracturing for oil and gas in the town. That Memo also requested that the Planning Board review the Hydrofracking Committee report and make zoning ordinance recommendations to the Town Board.

Upon receipt of the May 13, 2013 Memo, the following passages from official Planning Board meeting minutes confirm that the Planning Board not only acknowledged receiving the Hydrofracking Committee report containing the proposed zoning ordinance amendment, it actively proceeded to review the report in response to the Town Supervisor's request for zoning ordinance recommendations.

<u>May 21, 2013 Meeting</u>. "After some discussion it was clarified that the Town Supervisor requested that the Planning Board review the Hydrofracking Report and make suggestions regarding the preparation and implementation of zoning ordinances as recommended in the report presented to the Town Board and circulated to the Planning Board."

<u>June 18, 2013 Meeting</u>. "The Planning Board reviewed the request made by the Town Supervisor to review the Hydrofracking Committee's report. Also to take into account any additional

pertinent information generated by future research the Planning Board deems necessary to make a balanced and informed recommendation to the Town Board...The Planning Board will continue to study the issue of Gas Development and Hydro-fracking."

July 16, 2013 Meeting. "The Planning Board continues its Town Board requested review of the Hydrofracking Committee's report."

Unmentioned in the May 13, 2013 Memo, but clearly applicable to the Supervisor's request for advice from the Planning Board, is Colden's local law Chapter 108, Zoning, Article XXV, 108-130 B. That law stipulates the manner in which all zoning ordinance amendments referred to the Planning Board are to be processed, including the preparation of an advisory report to the Town Board.

Attached is a copy of the April 11, 2013 Hydrofracking Committee report *Gas Drilling in the Town of Colden* presented to the Town Board. The committee's recommendation to amend the town's zoning ordinance is found on page 24 and reads: "We recommend that the Town's zoning ordinance be amended to prohibit both HVHF (High Volume Hydraulic Fracturing) drilling activities for oil and gas, and the disposal of HVHF waste fluids from elsewhere, in the Town of Colden."

* * * * *

Paragraph 10 (continued). "No information is supplied in the complaint as to the language of the proposed amendment to the Town of Colden Zoning Code."

Response. Here the Defense Counsel attempts to persuade the court that the use of the term "proposed amendment" applies only to the final stage of the town's long zoning ordinance amendment process, at which time the actual drafting of zoning ordinance language would be prepared. In the absence of the yet to be drafted language, the Defense Counsel falsely claims

Chapter 108, Zoning, Article XXV, 108-130 B does not apply.

Defense Counsel supplies no evidence that the legislative intent of the Colden Town Board, when enacting Chapter 108, Zoning, Article XXV, 108-130 B, was to restrict its provisions directing the Planning Board's advisory duties to the final, written draft local law.

In fact, such a narrow interpretation of Chapter 108, Zoning, Article XXV, 108-130 B would leave the Town Board without crucial Planning Board review services and advice during the prior stages of the ordinance amendment process leading up to the final Town Board decision to authorize the Planning Board to incur the legal expenses associated with drafting language for a proposed local law for the Town Board's consideration.

Land use planners customarily use the term "proposed amendment" throughout the step-by-step zoning ordinance decision making process: (1.) From the initial awareness that a health or safety issue exists and a proposed amendment to the zoning ordinance may be required to address the issue; (2.) To an evaluation of the subject issue by the Planning Board to determine whether the proposed zoning ordinance amendment is technically supported by the Town's master land use plan; (3.) To an assessment by the Planning Board of the scope and possible content of such a proposed amendment; (4.) To a Planning Board recommendation to the Town Board that such a proposed amendment to the Town's zoning ordinance is needed; (5.) Only then would the Town Board consider authorizing the Planning Board to incur the attorney expenses needed to develop the legal language to convert the proposed amendment into a draft local law.

Since the Planning Board never advanced past step two above (the crux of the Misdemeanor Complaint filed on December 1, 2014), well before proposed amendment language would have been prepared, the Defense Counsel's claim that, "No information is supplied in the complaint to the language of the proposed amendment..." is a bogus premise—a begging the question fallacy—intended to convince the court that such language should have been supplied in the complaint when, in fact, it did not yet exist.

* * * * *

Paragraph 11. "The complaint does not state any factual information to support an argument that the Planning Board was to report to the Town Board regarding hydrofracking. Town Law 271(14) <u>requires</u> that the Town Board must pass a resolution to refer any general matter to the Planning Board. No factual information is included in the complaint regarding any such resolution for referral of a report on hydrofracking to the Planning Board. Such resolution would have been <u>required</u> to include the time frame for the Planning Board to submit its report. Additionally, without said resolution there is no time frame for the Planning Board to report back to the Town Board."

Response. This paragraph is not only misleading, it is also factually erroneous. The Defense Counsel wants the court to accept his unfounded premise that the complaint is invalid in the absence of a town board resolution referring the proposed amendment to the planning board. This is not the case.

Town Law 271(14) does not, as the Defense Counsel claims, "require" a Town Board resolution to refer the Hydrofracking Committee's report, including the report's recommendation for a proposed zoning amendment, to the Planning Board.

Town Law 271(14) reads: "The town board <u>may</u> by resolution provide for the reference of any matter or class of matters, other than those referred to in subdivision thirteen of this section to the planning board before final action is taken thereon by the town board or other office or officer of said town having final authority over said matter."

In fact, the May 13, 2013 Town Supervisor's Memo referring the Hydrofracking Committee's report to the Planning Board

was not contrary to Town Law 271(14), as suggested by the
Defense Counsel.

* * * * *

Paragraph 12. "Town of Colden Code 108-130 (B) requires
the Planning Board to provide the Town Board with an advisory
report stating reasons for recommending or opposing adoption
of a proposed amendment to the Town Zoning Code. In the in-
stant matter, there was no proposed amendment to the Town
Zoning Code referred by resolution of the Town Board to the
Planning Board."

Response. Again, as in Paragraph 11 above, the Defense
Counsel wants the court to accept his unfounded premise that
the complaint is invalid in the absence of a town board resolution referring the proposed amendment to the planning board.
This is not the case.

Town Law 271(14) does not, as the Defense Counsel claims,
"require" a Town Board resolution to refer the Hydrofracking
Committee's report, including the report's recommendation for
a proposed zoning amendment to the Planning Board.

Town Law 271(14) reads: "The town board <u>may</u> by resolution
provide for the reference of any matter or class of matters, other
than those referred to in subdivision thirteen of this section to
the planning board before final action is taken thereon by the
town board or other office or officer of said town having final
authority over said matter."

In fact, the May 13, 2013 Town Supervisor's Memo referring
the Hydrofracking Committee's report to the Planning Board
was not contrary to Town Law 271(14), as suggested by the
Defense Counsel.

* * * * *

Paragraph 13. "It is impossible for the defendant to lead the Planning Board through a review process of a proposed amendment to the Town Zoning Code where no proposed amendment is provided for review."

Response. Here the Defense Counsel once again attempts to persuade the court that the use of the term "proposed amendment" applies only to the final stage of the long ordinance amendment process at which time the actual draft zoning ordinance language would be prepared and that, in the absence of such language, Chapter 108, Zoning, Article XXV, 108-130 B does not apply.

Defense Counsel supplies no evidence that the legislative intent of the Colden Town Board, when enacting Chapter 108, Zoning, Article XXV, 108-130 B, was to restrict its provisions directing the Planning Board's advisory duties to the final, written draft local law.

In fact, such a narrow interpretation of Chapter 108, Zoning, Article XXV, 108-130 B would leave the Town Board without crucial Planning Board review services and advice during the prior ordinance amendment decision making steps preceding the final Town Board decision authorizing the Planning Board to incur the expenses associated with drafting language for a proposed local law for the Town Board's consideration.

Land use planners customarily use the term "proposed amendment" throughout the step-by-step zoning ordinance decision making process: (1.) From the initial awareness that a health or safety issue exists and a proposed amendment to the zoning ordinance may be required to address the issue; (2.) To an evaluation of the subject issue by the Planning Board to determine whether the proposed zoning ordinance amendment is technically supported by the Town's master land use plan; (3.) To an assessment by the Planning Board of the scope and possible content of such a proposed amendment; (4.) To a Planning Board recommendation to the Town Board that such a proposed amendment to the Town's zoning ordinance is needed; (5.) Only then would the Town Board consider authorizing the Planning Board to incur the attorney expenses needed to develop the legal language to convert the proposed amendment into a draft local law.

* * * * *

Summary. The subject Notice of Motion to Dismiss before the court is seriously flawed and not a reliable document upon which to decide whether or not to dismiss the subject Misdemeanor Complaint.

As the court considers whether to approve or reject the subject Notice of Motion to Dismiss, I urge the court to give the foregoing responses to that Motion a careful reading.

A just decision requires nothing less since, as alleged in the Misdemeanor Complaint, the documented conduct of the Town of Colden Planning Board has denied the people of the Town of Colden of their fundamental right to a local government based on the rule of law and due process.

* * * * *

On February 8, 2016, the Town of Boston court dismissed the case.

The district attorney, in a letter, said he did not oppose the dismissal, "because there was no time restriction in which the board is required to make a decision on matters submitted on for their review. The delay in the Planning Board deciding on this issue does not use a criminal charge."

* * * * *

New York Penal Law, Title L, Offenses Against Public Administration

Article 195, Official Misconduct

"A public official is guilty of official misconduct when, with intent to obtain a benefit or deprive another person of a benefit:

1. He commits an act relating to his office but constituting an unauthorized exercise of his official function, knowing that such act is unauthorized; or,

2. He knowingly refrains from performing a duty which is imposed upon him by law or is clearly inherent in the nature of his office.

Official misconduct is a class A misdemeanor."